ACT and SAT Test Prep: English, Reading, and Writing

Send all inquiries to:
McGraw-Hill Education
Two Penn Plaza
New York, New York 10121

ISBN: 978-0-07-682024-5 (Blue Edition)
MHID: 0-07-682024-6

Printed in the United States of America.

2 3 4 5 6 7 8 9 LHS 24 23 22 21 20 19

Contents

PART I

ACT Strategies and Concept Review

ACT English Test: Strategies and Concept Review

The ACT English Test is designed to measure your ability to understand and interpret the ACT's version of Standard Written English. As you are probably aware, English is a complex language with many variations. Major publications maintain "style sheets" for their employees to use so that they stay consistent over time and between writers. The ACT style sheet is not available as such. But, we've looked at every released exam we could for the past 25 years and we have included the rules that are rewarded by the ACT in this book. There may be a few differences from the rules that have been taught to you. And, you may be taught different rules by your professors once you get to college.

Each ACT English Test includes 5 passages with 15 questions each, for a total of 75 multiple-choice questions. The passages cover a variety of subjects, ranging from historical discussions to personal narratives. The questions are divided into two main categories: Usage/Mechanics questions and Rhetorical Skills questions. Usage/Mechanics questions test your basic English usage and grammar skills, while Rhetorical Skills questions test your ability to express an idea clearly and concisely. In this chapter, we'll give you useful strategies and techniques, an overview of the rules of grammar and punctuation that will be tested by Usage/Mechanics questions, and a breakdown of the writing skills tested by Rhetorical Skills questions. (You will find all of this information useful on the optional Writing Test also.)

GENERAL STRATEGIES AND TECHNIQUES

Use the following general strategies when tackling the ACT English Test.

Listen to Your Brain

Steve Says:

If all else is equal, you should lean toward the shortest answer.

This technique is known as "subvocalization" to psychologists. It means to turn on your internal narrator and "read aloud silently." You can usually trust your ears when answering many of the questions on the English Test. In other words, if it sounds right to you, it probably is. You will recognize when and how to apply basic rules of grammar, even if you don't recall what the specific rule is. You can tap into the part of your brain that controls language processing as you read. That part of your brain "knows" how English is supposed to sound. Let that part of your brain work for you. Remember, the ACT English Test does NOT require you to state a specific rule, only to apply it correctly.

Consider the following example:

Instead of studying for the exam. The students went to

a movie.

1

When you read this sentence to yourself, your brain is most likely going to recognize that the first sentence is a fragment. You will probably automatically combine both sentences. On the ACT, look for the answer choice that replaces the period with a comma.

Avoid Redundancy

Amy Says:

Skim the passage. If you have a general sense of the structure and overall meaning of the passage, you will be more likely to choose the correct answers on questions that ask about a specific part of the passage.

On the ACT English Test, wordiness and redundancy are never rewarded. Throughout the test, you will be asked to make choices that best express an idea. Usually, the fewer words that you use, the better. Be wary of words that have the same meaning being used in the same sentence. For example, it is not necessary to say "the tiny, little girl smiled at me." Both *tiny* and *little* have the same meaning, so using one or the other is sufficient.

Consider the following example:

Canadian currency usually looks and appears very

2

different from its American counterpart.

Because "looks" and "appears" mean the same thing, you can simply pick one of them to make the sentence better.

Take DELETE and NO CHANGE Seriously

You will sometimes see the answer choice "DELETE the underlined portion." Selecting this option will remove the underlined portion from the sentence or paragraph. "DELETE" is a viable answer choice when it eliminates redundant or irrelevant statements. When "DELETE" is given as an answer choice on the ACT, it is correct more than half of the time.

Consider the following example:

> It is important to be cautious and carefully plan your
>   3
>
> class schedule each semester.

While this sentence is grammatically correct, it contains redundancy. The underlined portion is not necessary to the sentence; in fact, the sentence is much more concise and logical without the underlined portion. When DELETE is offered as an answer choice, ask yourself whether or not the underlined portion is relevant and necessary to the general structure of the sentence. If it is not, DELETE may be your best choice.

On the ACT English Test, the first answer choice for almost every question is NO CHANGE. This answer choice should come up about as often as the others do on your answer sheet. Just because a portion of the passage is underlined doesn't mean that there is something wrong with it.

Consider the following example:

> The old man often fished the river that flowed past his
>   4
>
> cabin door.

This sentence does not require any changes. On the ACT, the answer choices to a question like this might include a different word, such as the past-form verb *passed*. Your job is to consider grammar, context, and word choice when selecting the best answer, and recognize when the sentence is best as written.

Steve Says:

Since there can only be one correct answer for each question, you can eliminate any two choices that mean the same as each other. If you find that two of the choices are synonyms, eliminate them both.

USAGE AND MECHANICS

This area of the ACT English Test addresses punctuation, grammar and usage, and sentence structure. The 40 Usage/Mechanics questions on the actual ACT ask you to apply the rules of Standard Written English to specific sections of the passage, which are usually underlined.

The following strategies and techniques, along with those mentioned on pages 10 through 12, should help you to move quickly and accurately through the Usage and Mechanics questions on the ACT English Test.

Try the Answer Choices

Because the test asks you to consider replacing the underlined portion, read each of the choices back into the sentence and select the one that is grammatically correct and/or clearly expresses the idea. If an answer choice creates an error in grammar or sounds awkward and wordy, eliminate it.

Consider the following examples:

We arrived home three weeks later <u>to witness</u> an incredible

                                          1

transformation; all of the water damage had been repaired!

   1. A. NO CHANGE
       B. by witnessing
       C. for the witnessing of
       D. to the witness of

The best answer is A. This sentence is correct as written. It is in the active voice and correctly uses the infinitive "to witness." Answer choice B suggests that witnessing the transformation was the method by which the author arrived home, which doesn't make sense. Answer choices C and D are awkward when read back into the sentence and do not effectively convey the intended idea. Because answer choice A is clear, concise, and error-free, it is the best choice.

I removed a picture from the <u>box and placed</u> it in the

                                                         2

photo album.

      Which of the following alternatives to the underlined portion would NOT be acceptable?

2. F. box and then placed
   G. box; then I placed
   H. box, placed
   J. box, placing

The best answer is H. When you read each of the answer choices back into the original sentence, the only one that does NOT work is "box, placed." This selection creates an incomplete sentence. The remaining answer choices are grammatically correct and clearly express the intended idea.

Amy Says:

Pay attention to apostrophes—you can often eliminate incorrect answer choices by quickly deciding whether an apostrophe is necessary.

Simplify the Answer Choices

Sometimes you can quickly eliminate incorrect answer choices by showing that one part of an answer choice is incorrect; if one part is wrong, the whole thing is wrong. Simplify the answer choices by focusing on one part at a time.

Consider the following examples:

My English teacher gave us daily quizzes, which angered and confused us. Soon, the teachers' motives became clear.
                    1

1. A. NO CHANGE
   B. teachers motives
   C. teacher's motives
   D. teacher's motive's

The best answer is C. The first step in answering this question is to determine how many teachers are there. The previous sentence says "My English teacher," so there is only one teacher. Therefore, you can eliminate answer choices A and B, which include the plural form of the noun "teacher." Because both answer choices C and D include the singular possessive form, you can assume that is the correct form of the noun; move on to the word "motives." You simply have to decide whether the plural form or the singular possessive form is correct. In this case, the plural form is best—the teacher has more than one motive—so answer choice C must be correct. The singular possessive form "motive's" is not correct because no possession is indicated.

My dog ran away and lost its collar.
                         2

2. F. NO CHANGE
   G. lost it's
   H. lost its'
   J. losing it's

The best answer is F. The first step in quickly answering this question is to focus on the pronoun. Because the collar belongs to the dog, the possessive form "its" is correct, and you can eliminate answer choices G and J, which include the contraction of "it is," and answer choice H, which is never correct. (You know that s' generally indicates plural possession; "it" is a singular pronoun and can never show plural possession.) By simplifying the answer choices you are able to quickly and accurately select the correct answer. Additionally, if you knew for certain that "its" was correct, a quick glance at the answer choices would reveal that answer choice F was the only viable option.

Don't Make New Mistakes

Because this test is timed, your tendency might be to rush through some of the seemingly more simple Usage and Mechanics questions. Be careful not to select an answer choice that introduces a new error to the sentence.

Consider the following examples:

While <u>they're, he had as</u> one of his counselors Steve, his friend's older brother.
      1

1. **A.** NO CHANGE
   B. they're
   C. there,
   D. there, he had as

The best answer is D. Because "they're" is the contraction of "they are," you can eliminate answer choices A and B. You might have been tempted to select the shortest, most concise answer, which would be answer choice C. However, this choice creates a sentence fragment.

Attending a large university has taught me to understand and appreciate <u>differently cultures from</u> my own.
      2

2. **F.** NO CHANGE
   G. cultures different then
   H. cultures different from
   J. cultures differently by

The best answer is H. The context of the sentence suggests a contrast between the writer's culture and those cultures that are different. Be careful not to misread answer choice G and select it—"then" indicates a time, not a contrast. Answer choices F and J are awkward and use the adverb "differently" to modify the verbs "understand" and "appreciate," instead of the adjective "different" to modify the noun "cultures."

RHETORICAL SKILLS

This area of the ACT English Test addresses writing strategy, organization, and style. Rhetoric can be defined as "effective and persuasive use of language." The 35 Rhetorical Skills questions assess your ability to make choices about the effectiveness and clarity of a word, phrase, sentence, or paragraph. You may also be asked about the English passage as a whole. Most of the Rhetorical Skills questions are referred to by a number in a box. The following is more information on the three main categories of Rhetorical Skills questions, Strategy, Organization, and Style:

Strategy: *The choices made and methods used by an author when composing or revising an essay.*

The ACT English Test measures your ability to recognize several areas of writing strategy, including the flow of ideas; the appropriateness and purpose of both the passage and elements of the passage; and the effectiveness of opening, transitional, and closing sentences.

Take a look at the following sample Strategy question:

> Horseback riding requires less skill than many people think. Granted, not just anyone can hop onto the back of a horse and maneuver the animal around a racetrack or jumping course, but many people can sit comfortably in a saddle for a short period of time while a horse calmly walks along a wooded trail. [1]

1. The writer wishes to add information here that will further support the point made in the preceding sentence. Which of the following sentences will do that best?

   A. Saddles are designed for specific purposes, such as pleasure riding, barrel racing, and roping.
   B. Each year, thousands of people who have never before been on a horse enjoy guided, one-hour trail rides.
   C. Even experienced riders enjoy the peace and tranquility of a ride through the woods after a long day of training.
   D. Former racehorses are often used as trail horses when they retire from the track.

1. The best answer is B. To correctly answer this question, you must first determine the point made in the preceding sentence. The main point of the sentence is that many people, even if they are not skilled at horseback riding, can ride at a slow pace for a short period of time. Answer choice B best supports that idea by providing information about the large number of first-time riders who enjoy relatively short trail rides.

Organization: *Developing logical sequences, categorizing elements, ranking items in order, identifying main ideas, making connections, writing introductions and conclusions, and resolving problems within an essay.*

Organization questions on the ACT English Test are designed to test issues related to the organization of ideas within a passage, the most logical order of sentences and paragraphs, and the relevance of statements made within the context of the passage.

The following is an example of an Organization question:

[1] Prior to this, my mother had stated that she and my dad would only be staying with me for three days. [2] As adults, we often have mixed feelings about a visit from our parents—while we are happy to see them, we also hope that their stay is for a definite and short period of time. [3] My parents recently planned a trip to my neck of the woods, and I prepared my humble home for their arrival. [4] They showed up on the appointed day and my mother announced that they would stay for a full week.

2. Which of the following sequences of sentences will make this paragraph most logical?
   F. NO CHANGE
   G. 1, 4, 3, 2
   H. 2, 3, 4, 1
   J. 4, 3, 2, 1

2. The best answer is H. The best approach to this type of question is to determine which sentence should come first. The first sentence of a paragraph usually introduces the topic of the paragraph. In this case, the sentence that provides us with information about the topic of the paragraph is sentence [2]. Therefore, the first sentence in the logical sequence of this paragraph is sentence [2]. Because the only answer choice that places sentence [2] in the first position is answer choice H, that must be the correct choice. By positioning one sentence at a time you will be able to eliminate answer choices until only the correct one remains.

Style: *The author's presentation of the written word, usually either formal or informal.*

Good writing involves effective word choice as well as clear and unambiguous expression. The ACT English Test requires you to recognize and eliminate redundant material, understand the tone of the passage, and make sure that the ideas are expressed clearly and succinctly.

The following Style questions focus on these issues:

> While <u>having the appearance</u> to be a simple game, checkers is actually quite
>   3
> complicated. Mathematically there are about 500 quintillion possible ways to win the
>
> game. Despite this, checkers continues to be mostly a fun game for those who play it,
>
> even at the competitive level. <u>Checkers was first played in the twelfth century</u>. Some
>   4
> of the classic moves used in competitions have names like the Goose Walk, Duffer's
>
> Delight, and the Boomerang. With names like these, it seems <u>that even a serious game</u>
>   5
> has its own sense of humor.

3. **A.** NO CHANGE
   B. appearing
   C. appearing that
   D. appearances show it

4. **F.** NO CHANGE
   G. First played in the twelfth century was checkers.
   H. Checkers was originally from the twelfth century.
   J. DELETE the underlined portion.

5. **A.** NO CHANGE
   B. crucial that a serious game
   C. that such a serious game
   D. in all seriousness, a game

3. The best answer is B. By replacing the underlined portion with each answer choice you can see that the best way to express this idea is simply with the word *appearing*, answer choice B. Remember to trust the way that things "sound," and go for the shortest, most simple way to say something.

4. The best answer is J. Although the sentence as it is used is grammatically correct, it does not fit the context of the paragraph. In other words, it is irrelevant information and should be omitted; answer choice J is correct.

5. The best answer is A. This question asks you to look at the choice and function of the words in the sentence. The tone of the paragraph is informational, yet informal. A word like *crucial* does not fit the context; therefore, answer choice B should be eliminated. Answer choices C and D do not really fit the context of the paragraph either. The sentence as it is written fits best within the style and tone of the passage, so answer choice A is correct.

ACT Reading Test: Strategies and Concept Review

The ACT Reading Test has four passages of about 700–900 words each that are each followed by ten questions, for a total of forty questions. The questions can be answered based on information found in the passages. There is virtually no prior knowledge tested on the Reading Test. You will have 35 minutes to complete your work on this section.

The test authors choose subject matter that they think represent the type of material that you will have to read in college. All of the passages on the actual ACT come from material that has been previously published. Therefore, you can rely on the fact that the passages are well edited and will be correct in terms of their grammar, punctuation, and overall structure.

The four passages will be of four different types, as follows:

1. **Prose Fiction** (excerpts from novels and short stories)
2. **Humanities** (passages with topics from arts and literature, often biographies of famous authors, artists, musicians, etc.)
3. **Social Studies** (History, Sociology, Psychology, and other areas of Social Science)
4. **Natural Sciences** (Biology, Chemistry, Physics, etc.)

Your ACT score report will include an overall scaled score, which comes from your total number of correct answers out of forty, and subscores for Social Studies/Sciences, which combines your performance on the Social Science and Natural Science passages. There is also a subscore given for Arts/Literature, which is derived from the twenty questions on Prose Fiction and Humanities. The subscores are then manipulated to arrive at your scaled score.

Your two subscores might not add up just exactly to your Reading score, but they will be very close.

TIMING

If you choose to answer all of the questions on the Reading Test, you will have about eight minutes to work on each of the four passages and still have enough time to mark the answers on your answer sheet. For many students, it makes sense to slow down a bit to focus on two or three of the passages and simply guess on the remaining questions. Whether you choose to work on all four of the passages will depend on where you are on the scoring scale. If you get 30 out of the 40 questions correct, you end up with a scaled Reading score of about a 29. (There is minor variation in scaled scores from one exam to the next.) A score of 29 on the Reading Test means that your Reading score would be well within the top 10% of Reading scores nationwide.

The national average ACT Reading Test score is around a 20 or 21 on the 36-point scale. This means that the average ACT-taker gets just about exactly one half of the questions correct on the Reading Test. Of course, we recommend that you strive to do your best and we hope that all readers of this book will be well into the above-average range on the ACT. However, it pays to be realistic about what is possible for you on test day. If, after a reasonable amount of practice and study you are still able to tackle only three of the four passages comfortably within the 35 minutes you are given, you are not in very bad shape. If you can get most of those thirty questions correct, and pick up a few correct answers by guessing on the remaining ten, you could still realistically hope to end up with a top 10% score on the Reading Test.

If you are closer to the average ACT Reading test-taker and find that you are only able to really understand two passages and their accompanying questions in the time allowed, you are still likely to get credit for a few more correct responses by guessing on the remaining twenty questions. In fact, since there are four answer choices for each question, you should predict that you would get about 25% correct when guessing at random. This means that guessing on twenty questions should yield about five correct answers. If you manage to get only 15 correct of the 20 questions that go with the two passages that you work on carefully, you would still have a scaled score of approximately 20 or 21.

Most students should not attempt all four of the passages on the Reading Test and should choose a passage or two that will be "sacrificed" in the interest of time management. There are a few factors to consider when deciding which passage(s) you will sacrifice. For example, you should certainly look at the subject matter. Most students have distinct preferences for one or two of the passage types mentioned previously. Conversely, there is probably at least one type of passage that always seems to account for the bulk of the questions that you miss on practice Reading Tests. Always remember to answer every question on your answer sheet, even if you are guessing.

While vocabulary is not tested directly on the ACT, there is certainly an advantage to knowing what the words mean as you try to decipher a passage.

Steve Says:

Let your practice testing help you to decide whether to attack all four passages. If you decide to focus on two or three passages on test day, let your practice help guide you when deciding which passages to sacrifice.

GENERAL STRATEGIES AND TECHNIQUES

Use the following general strategies when tackling the ACT Reading Test.

Read the Question Stems First

Once you have decided to attack a specific passage, you should have a plan for *how* to do it. The single most powerful strategy for the Reading Test is to read the *question stems* first. The question stems are the prompts, or stimuli, that appear before the four answer choices. Don't read the answer choices before you read the passage. Most of the answer choices are wrong and, in fact, are referred to by testing professionals as *distractors*. If you read them before you read the passage, you are much more likely to be confused. The questions themselves, though, may contain useful information. You may find that the questions repeatedly refer to specific names or terms. You will find other questions that contain references to the line numbers that are printed down the left side of the passage. These can be very useful in focusing your attention and energy on the parts of the passage that are likely to lead to correct answers to questions.

Don't "Study" the Passage

Probably the biggest mistake that you could make is to read these passages as though you are studying for a test. Unlike most of your previous exams, the ACT Reading Test (and the Science Test also) is in an open-book format. The open-book aspect of the Reading Test means that you should read efficiently. You should not read slowly and carefully as though you will have to remember the information for hours or days. Instead, you should read loosely and only dwell on information that you are sure is important because you need it to answer a question.

The test writers are not interested in whether you can store information for a long period of time and then recall it on an exam day or weeks later. Your reading should be very goal-oriented. If the information you are looking at does not help to answer a question that the test writers find important, then you should not linger over it.

When you study for a test, you probably read carefully so that you don't miss some detail or subtle nuance that is likely to help you to answer an exam question later. You probably reread any part of the material that doesn't make sense immediately. You probably also make connections to your prior knowledge, visualizing as much as you can. If you find a new word, you probably slow down or stop reading and try to figure out what the word means by using context clues. You might also underline or highlight important-looking facts, or make margin notes to help you understand and recall information when you review later.

All of these skills are very useful for the type of reading that you must do when preparing for most exams. However, they are not very useful in the context of the ACT Reading Test. In fact, if you read these passages in the same way that you read when you are studying for a closed-book exam, you are falling into some of the traps that are set by the psychometricians.

Amy Says:

The best scores on this section are usually earned by students who have two key skills: paraphrasing and skimming. Paraphrasing means to put things in your own words, which will help you to understand what the question is really asking. Skimming will help you to get through the material more quickly.

The test writers know a lot about how the human mind works. They know about something called *negative transference of learning* that occurs when we have skills that are "adaptive" or useful in our environment. But, when the environment changes, and we keep using our old skills, they can be "maladaptive," or harmful.

So, you should take stock of your current reading habits, compare them to the strategies explained below, and make changes where you must in order to achieve a higher ACT score. Don't feel that you have to give up all of the reading skills that you have acquired thus far in your educational career. However, it is a good idea to add to your "tool box" so that you can adapt your approach to the requirements of the reading "environment" in which you find yourself.

Read for the Main Idea

"Main Idea" has three components: "What?," "What About It?," and "Why did the author write this?" If you can answer these three questions, then you understand the main idea.

Too often, students confuse *topic* with main idea. The topic of a passage only answers the question of "What is the passage about?" If that is all that you notice, you are missing some very important information.

For example, consider a passage that has a topic that we are all at least somewhat familiar with: rain forests. Let's say that you are faced with one passage that is about the ongoing destruction of the rain forests and includes a call for the reader to get involved and help to stop the destruction in some way. "What?" = rain forests. "What About It?" = destruction. "Why?" = to inspire the reader to take action.

Now, say that we keep the same topic, rain forests, but change the other two dimensions: "What About It?" = biodiversity (species variation). "Why?" = to educate the reader. Then we are reading a very different passage. You need all three dimensions of the main idea to understand all that you need to answer the questions correctly.

So, read a little more slowly at the beginning until you get a grip on the main idea. Then, you can skim the rest of the passage.

Skim the Passage

Don't underline. Don't use context clues. When you come to a word or phrase that is unfamiliar, just blow past it. There will be time to come back if you need to. But there is a strong chance that you won't need to bother figuring out exactly what that one word or phrase means in order to answer the bulk of the ten questions that follow the passage. If you waste some of your precious time, you will never get it back. This habit can be hard to break. With perseverance and practice, you will become comfortable with a less-than-perfect understanding of the passage.

The goal at this stage is to develop a general understanding of the structure of the passage so that you can find what you are looking for when you refer

---

Steve Says:

The Main Idea ("Big Picture") actually has three parts:

1. Topic—what is the passage about?
2. Scope—what aspect of the topic is being discussed?
3. Purpose—why was the passage written?

Identify all three parts to easily answer "Big Picture" questions.

back to the passage. You should pay attention to paragraph breaks and quickly try to determine the subtopic for each one. The first sentence is not always the topic sentence. So, don't believe those who say that you can read the first and last sentence of each paragraph and skip the rest of the sentences completely. You are better off skimming over all of the words even if you end up forgetting most of what you read almost immediately.

Remember that you can write in your test booklet. So, when you see a topic word, circle it. If you can sum up a paragraph in a word or two, jot it down in the margin. Remember that the idea at this stage is to not waste time. Keep moving through the material.

Read and Answer the Questions

Start at the beginning of each group of questions. Read the question and make sure that you understand it. Paraphrase it if you need to. (This means to put the question into your own words.) If you paraphrase, keep your language simple. Pretend you are "translating" the question to an average eighth grader. If you can make sure that the person you are imagining can understand the question, then you are ready to answer it. Use the following strategies when answering Reading Test questions:

Refer Back to the Passage

Go back to the part of the passage that will probably contain the answer to your question. It is true that some of the questions on the ACT ask you to draw conclusions based on the information that you read. However, even these questions should be answered based on the information in the passage. There will always be some strong hints, or evidence, that will lead you to an answer.

Some of the questions contain references to specific lines of the passage. The trick in those cases is to read a little before and a little after the specific line that is mentioned. At least read the entire sentence that contains the line that is referenced.

Some of the questions don't really tell you where to look for the answer, or they are about the passage as a whole. In these cases, think about what you learned about the passage while you were skimming it. Note the subtopics for the paragraphs, and let them guide you to the part of the passage that contains the information you need.

Don't be afraid to refer back to the passage repeatedly, and don't be reluctant to skip around within the ten-question group that accompanies each of the four passages. In fact, many students report success with a strategy of actually skipping back and forth among passages. This plan will not work for everyone. But if you feel comfortable with it after trying it on practice tests, then we can't think of any reason not to do it on test day.

> **Amy Says:**
>
> One of the important skills rewarded by the ACT is the ability to sift through text to find the word or concept that you need. This skill improves with practice.

Predict an Answer

After you have found the relevant information in the passage, try to answer the question in your mind. Do this before you look at the answer choices. Remember: three out of every four answer choices are incorrect. Not only are they incorrect, but they were written by experts to confuse you. They are less likely to confuse you if you have a clear idea of an answer before you read the answer choices. If you can predict an answer for the question, then skim the choices presented and look for your answer. You may have to be a little flexible to recognize it. Your answer may be there dressed up in different words. If you can recognize a restatement of your predicted answer, mark it. The odds that you will manage to predict one of the incorrect answer choices are slim. Mark the question if you are unsure. If there is time, you can come back to it later.

Use the Process of Elimination

The process of elimination is a good tool, although it should not be the only tool in your box. It is reliable but slow. Use it as a backup strategy either when you cannot predict an answer for a question or your prediction is not listed as an answer choice.

It can be hard to break the habit of applying the process of elimination to every question. You likely have "overused" this technique because you have had more than enough time to take tests in the past.

As mentioned previously, the ACT has time limits that are not even realistic for most students. Form some new reading habits by practicing with ACT reading passages under realistic conditions.

QUESTION TYPES

The ACT Reading Test includes the following question types:

1. **Main Idea/Point of View.** These questions may ask about the main idea of the passage or a specific paragraph. They may also ask about the author's point of view or perspective, and the intended audience.

2. **Specific Detail.** These questions can be as basic as asking you about a fact that is readily found by referring to a part of the passage. Often, specific detail questions are a bit more difficult because they ask you to interpret the information that is referred to.

3. **Conclusion/Inference.** These questions require the test-taker to put together information from the passage to use it as evidence for a conclusion. You will have to find language in the passage that will lead you to arrive at the inference that the question demands. (To "infer" is to draw a conclusion based on information in the passage.)

4. **Extrapolation.** These questions ask you to go beyond the passage itself and find answers that are *probably* true based on what you know from the passage. They can be based on the author's tone or on detailed information in the passage.

5. **Vocabulary in Context.** The ACT does not have a separate vocabulary test. However, there are occasional questions that ask what a specific word means from the passage. The context of the passage should lead you to an educated guess even if you don't know the specific word being asked about.

STRATEGIES FOR SPECIFIC QUESTION TYPES

Practice sufficiently to be able to identify the different question types and apply the appropriate strategies.

Main Idea

Answer according to your understanding of the three components of the main idea that were mentioned previously (What? What About It? and Why?). It is also worth noting that the incorrect choices are usually either too broad or too narrow in scope. You should eliminate the answer choices that focus on a specific part of the passage and also eliminate the choices that are too general and could describe other passages besides the one that you are working on.

Specific Detail

Refer back to the passage to find the answer to the question. Use line or paragraph references in the questions, if they are given. Recognize that sometimes the answer choices are paraphrased, so don't just choose the answers that contain words that appeared in the passage. Make sure that the choice you select responds to the question.

Conclusion/Inference

Although you have to do a bit of thinking for these questions, you should be able to find very strong evidence for your answer. If you find yourself creating a long chain of reasoning and including information from outside the passage, stop and reconsider. The ACT rewards short, strong connections between the evidence in the passage and the answer that is credited.

Extrapolation

This question type asks you about what is probably true based on information in the passage. You need to be sensitive to any clues about the author's tone or attitude and any clues about how the characters in the passage feel. Eliminate any choices that are outside the scope of the passage. As with Inference questions above, the ACT rewards concise, strong connections between the passage and the correct answers.

Vocabulary in Context

The ACT only asks a few vocabulary questions, and they are always in the context of a passage. The best way to answer these questions is the simplest way: just read the answer choices back into the sentence mentioned in the question stem and choose the one that changes the meaning of the sentence the least. If you recognize the Latin roots of the words, or if you have knowledge of Italian, Spanish, or French and recognize roots, you can make educated guesses.

ACT Writing Test: Strategies and Review

The ACT Writing Test is optional, meaning that students can choose whether to take it. Make your decision based on the requirements of the colleges and universities to which you plan to apply. Be sure to check with your schools of choice before registering for the ACT. If you take the Writing Test, it will come at the end of the ACT exam. You will have a short break between the ACT multiple-choice sections and the Writing Test.

The Writing Test consists of a "prompt," which is a brief discussion of a topic to which you must respond, and some blank, lined space in which to write your answer. You will have forty minutes to complete the test. The graders are not looking for long essay answers; they are looking for quality essays.

You will receive a total of five scores for your Writing Test: a single subject-level writing score reported on a range of 2–12 and four domain scores. The four domains are "Ideas and Analysis," "Development and Support," "Organization," and "Language Use and Conventions." Each of the four domains is also scored from 2–12. Two professional, trained readers will score your essay on a scale of 1–6 in each of the four writing domains. If the readers' scores disagree by more than one point, a third reader will evaluate the essay and that reader's score will be doubled. The readers are guided by these descriptions of the domains:

Ideas and Analysis: This domain reflects the candidate's ability to engage critically with multiple perspectives and generate relevant ideas.

Development and Support: This domain reflects the ability to construct a sound argument that is well supported by examples.

Organization: This domain reflects the ability to organize and express ideas clearly and with purpose while guiding the reader through discussion.

Language Use and Conventions: This domain reflects the use of language following the rules and conventions of style, grammar, syntax, word choice, and mechanics, including proper punctuation.

If you do not take the Writing Test, your Composite Score (overall multiple-choice score) will not be affected, but the separate English Language Arts (ELA) score will not be reported. Please visit **www.act.org** for more details on the scoring system.

The most important thing to know about this essay is that THERE IS NO CORRECT ANSWER! The readers are looking at the essay as an example of your ability to write a clear, concise, persuasive piece. DO NOT WASTE TIME by trying to figure out which position the test writers want you to choose.

This part of the ACT is designed to measure your writing skills. The test writers specifically choose topics that are probably relevant to high school students, and they even give a couple of different points of view from which to choose. They are looking for essays that have a clear position and support it. The graders will reward you with more points if you stay focused on your main idea throughout your essay and back up your position by giving specific examples and information. You will certainly do well if you have a clear, logical structure and if your language is correct and free of errors in grammar or vocabulary. Don't take any vocabulary risks when writing this essay. If you are not sure what a word means, don't use it. It should go without saying, but remember that you should not fill your essay with slang, jargon, or profanity.

There is a great overlap between the English section of the ACT and the Writing Test. If you can recognize proper English and point out common errors on the multiple-choice portion of the ACT, you should be able to avoid making those same errors on the Writing Test.

The essay prompt gives you three different positions on the issue. You will be given some scratch paper for this part of the ACT. Later in the chapter, we will discuss some specific ideas for the best way to use it. Be certain that you do use it. This is not the time to jump in and start writing a stream-of-consciousness, shoot-from-the-hip answer off the top of your head. Even though you do not have time to do a full first and second draft of this essay, make use of the time that is given to you to do some pre-writing. Be sure that you plan out what you are going to say before you actually start writing out your final answer.

At this point in your ACT testing day, you are likely to be somewhat tired. Try to focus on the fact that you are almost finished, and do what you can to keep your focus for the last thirty minutes. In some cases, this essay will be important to people who make admissions decisions at the institutions to which you are applying.

Amy Says:

Get a "fresh pair" of eyes to review your practice essays. It will not take long for an experienced reader to give you valuable feedback.

HOW TO PREPARE

As was noted earlier in this book, humans acquire skills through practice. Since the Writing Test is a test of your writing skills, you should practice writing in order to score better. Specifically, you should practice the type of writing that is rewarded by the scoring rubric. The best way to make sure that you are on track is to have someone with experience in this area, someone you trust, give you specific feedback on the good and not-so-good parts of your practice essays. You can gain from reading your own essays and comparing them to a rubric. However, writers tend to develop blind spots when it comes to areas that need improvement in their own essays. It is always a good idea to get a fresh set of eyes to review your work. Most high school teachers would be delighted if a student came to them for help on a practice essay. It does not take long for an experienced grader to give feedback that can be immensely valuable to a student.

THE ESSAY PROMPT

The prompt will be a few sentences long and will mention an issue that can cause some disagreement. It will also include three different positions on the issue and then instructions to take a position on the issue in your essay. The page following the prompt will be blank on both sides, except for a note that says that anything that you put on those two pages will not be scored. This is the "scratch paper" on which you can jot down whatever notes you want to and do some outlining to help keep yourself on track as you write in your answer document.

Four pages of lined answer space follow the blank pages. You are to confine your response to these four pages. It may not sound like a lot of space, but we have found that the students who write the most and complain about not having enough room to finish are usually spending too much time on irrelevant discussion or have needless repetition in their answers. You may use pencil only. No ink is allowed. You should probably write with a medium pressure since, if you don't press hard enough, your words might not scan. If you press too hard, you will have a hard time keeping your essay neat if you need to erase.

The prompt essentially describes a debate on an issue about which you are likely to have some strong feelings. If you do have strong feelings, you should just stick with your first response to the issue and work from there. If you don't, the fact that ACT will give you three different responses to the issue that other people have had means that you can just choose one of them as your starting point.

ESSAY WRITING TECHNIQUES

Here are the steps that are likely to result in the best essay that you can write. The steps are laid out so that you can perform them one at a time. This is not the time for "multitasking." If you were simply to read the stimulus and then try to write your answer out from the beginning to the end on the lined pages, you would certainly be doing several tasks at once. You would be creating the logical structure of your essay, searching your memory banks for vocabulary words, and anticipating counterarguments at the same time that you would be trying to apply the rules of grammar, punctuation, and spelling correctly, as well as remembering some good, relevant examples to plug into your essay structure. In short, those students who try to write without planning are setting themselves up for a score that is less than their potential because they are trying to do too many things at one time. Consider the following:

Read the Prompt

It is okay to read the prompt over more than once to be certain that you understand it completely. The test booklet is a resource for you to consume, so don't be afraid to underline, circle, and so on. The stimulus is short, so reading carefully will not take up much of your time. However, it may save you from making a mistake in responding to the prompt.

You must know what the task is before you begin. Rushing through this step can cost valuable points and make some of your hard work worthless.

One or two minutes will probably be sufficient time to read the prompt carefully.

Think About the Prompt

If the topic is something that you have thought about or discussed in the past, then you may already have an opinion. If not, then take a short time to formulate your opinion. This is what these essays are really all about: opinion. That is why there is really no correct or incorrect position to take. The test writers are careful to choose topics that have several sides that can be argued successfully. Remember that one of the characteristics of the rubric is taking a position on the issue. This is not the time to be overly diplomatic. Take a side and defend your choice.

This thinking process should not take very long, a few minutes at most.

Steve Says:

The planning stage is the most important stage of the essay-writing process. You can take up to 10 minutes to organize your position and examples and still probably have enough time to finish your essay.

Plan Your Essay

Your essay should begin with a clear statement of your position on the issue. There should be no doubt in the reader's mind about which side you are on from the beginning of your essay. You should use the scratch paper that is provided to outline the structure of your essay, beginning with your position statement.

There is an old saying about effective essays: "Tell them what you are going to tell them. Tell them. Then, tell them what you told them." In other words, you should have a clear introduction, a body, and a conclusion that echoes the introduction. You may choose to do a traditional five-paragraph essay, but it is possible to write a very effective essay with more paragraphs or fewer.

Your outline does not have to include complete sentences. It does have to include the ideas that you will put into your final draft. You need to be sure that you have a clear picture of where you are going and how you will get there before you start to write on the answer document.

You will hear some of the other test-takers around you scratching furiously with their pencils from the beginning of the 40-minute period. Sometimes that sound can make you feel like you are falling behind. You are not. Forty minutes is a long time to write two to four pages on a one-paragraph stimulus. The planning stage is the most important stage. Even if you spend 10 minutes on this stage, you will probably still be able to finish on time. Your essay will certainly be better than if you had simply started writing your thoughts with no planning.

Write Your Essay Out on the Answer Pages

You should also remember that there are really four categories of information when you are writing a persuasive essay and the opposing positions are clearly understood:

1. Positive for your position
2. Negative for your position
3. Positive for the opposing positions
4. Negative for the opposing positions

An effective essay uses facts from all four categories. You can think of your position as "correct" and the other positions as "incorrect." When you write a paragraph that is focused on the "correct" side of the issue, you should mention at least one aspect of your choice that may be seen as a negative by some people. Your essay will be much more persuasive if you do not ignore potential problems with your side of the debate. Of course, you should be sure to mention plenty of positive information in order to overcome the potential downside to which you are admitting.

The same technique can be applied to the part of your essay where you discuss opposing positions. You should admit that the other side of the debate has at least one strong point. Then, follow up with enough discussion of the pitfalls associated with the other side of the argument that your side ends up looking like the clear winner.

This is known as dealing with counterarguments, and it is the most effective way of presenting a persuasive written argument. To do this properly requires certain transition words. There are four basic categories of transition words that you will probably have to use:

Contrast: *But, However, On the other hand, Conversely, Although, Even though,* etc.
Similarity: *Likewise, Similarly, Also, Equally,* etc.
Evidence: *Since, Because, In light of, First, Second, Third,* etc.
Conclusion: *Therefore, Thus, As a result, So, It follows that, In conclusion,* etc.

An example of a sentence structure that will allow you to deal with these positive and negative categories of facts follows:

> *The opposition makes a valid point regarding the initial cost of my solution; the truth is that my solution would only cost a few dollars more per user than their option would. Furthermore, it would result in significant maintenance savings over the long run that would more than make up for the slightly higher start-up costs.*

This pair of sentences effectively deals in two ways with the potential objection that the other side might raise. First, it reduces the impact of the higher cost of the author's proposal by pointing out that the difference really is not very large when considered as a cost per user. Then, it points out that the costs will be recaptured in the future through increased savings. In addition, the sentence makes proper use of a semicolon. A semicolon is used correctly when you could erase it and replace it with a period and a capital letter. In other words, the semicolon links two independent clauses, which could stand alone as sentences in their own right. You should use the semicolon when the two sentences are very closely related and are continuing the same thought.

COMMON MISTAKES

There are many common errors that students make on the ACT Writing Test essay. If you know what to avoid, you will not only be a better writer, but, you will have a much easier time on the multiple-choice English Test. Consider the following:

Too General

The scoring rubric awards points for specific examples. Think of the best teachers you have had. They tend to tell you the general concept that they are teaching and then give one or more specific, memorable examples. This strategy works because of the memorable examples.

If you are told that there is no progress without determination and hard work, you might accept the statement as true and you may even remember it. However, you will have a much better chance of fully grasping the idea and remembering it later if you are given a specific example like Thomas Edison, who tried thousands and thousands of different filament materials in his lightbulbs before finally settling on one that gave acceptable light and lasted a reasonable period of time.

Too often, students make broad, general statements in their essays without giving any specific support. Make sure that you provide clear, simple examples of the general statements that you make.

Too Emotional and Opinionated

While it is true that the stimulus will be asking you for an opinion, you should not make the entire essay about your feelings. You should state what your opinion is and then back up your opinion with well-reasoned, logical support. Tell the reader *why* you feel the way you do rather than just telling *how* you feel.

Also, exclamation points are rarely appropriate for a Writing Test essay. Smiley faces or other "emoticons" are never appropriate.

Too Complicated

Many coaches and teachers have suggested that students apply the K.I.S.S. principle. While there is a slightly less polite formulation, we'll explain the K.I.S.S. principle as an acronym for "Keep It Short and Sweet." For example, do not use three words when one will do.

To illustrate, if you want to say, "I do not think that the proposal will work," do not write, "I believe that my feelings on this matter are correct when I state plainly and clearly that the previously proposed solution to this complicated problem will be somewhat less than completely effective as compared to other potential solutions, which have been brought forth concurrently."

The graders are not going to be blown away by your amazing ability to use a dozen words to state a plain idea. They are going to be blown away if you are able to make your point cleanly and clearly.

Amy Says:

Be sure to explain the connection between the examples that you use and your conclusion. Don't assume that the grader will agree with your viewpoint regarding the significance of a given fact.

Risky Vocabulary

If you are not sure what a word means or whether it would be appropriate to use in your essay, don't use it. Many an otherwise wonderful essay has been sunk by a word or two used incorrectly, which made the grader start to question the author's abilities.

For instance, if you were grading an essay that said, "High school students are often *condemned* for their kindness," you might know that the author meant to say, "High school students are often *commended* for their kindness." But you would still have to note the error and take it into account in scoring the essay.

Poor Handwriting

As mentioned previously in the chapter, the grader has to assign a score to your essay that depends on the grader's interpretation of the terms in the rubric. In order to help the grader interpret those terms in your favor when he or she is making judgment calls, you should write or print as neatly as you can. Make it easy for the graders to find the good things about your essay that will allow them to give you all of the points that your hard work deserves.

Shaky Logic

The essay that you must write for the Writing Test is an argument. It is an essay written with the purpose of defending a position. That position is your conclusion, and the support you are offering is evidence for that conclusion. There should be a cause-and-effect relationship between your evidence and your conclusion. In other words, the body of your essay should lead the reader to see the wisdom of your position.

For example, if you are taking the position in your essay that students should be subject to an 11:00 P.M. curfew, do not spend time discussing how you felt about your bedtime when you were seven years old.

Choose relevant examples that are connected to your position in a direct way. One way to do this is to use examples that point out the benefits of your position. For example, "I believe that anyone under the age of 18 should have an 11:00 P.M. curfew on school nights. This is because school starts at 8:00 A.M., which means that most students have to get up at 7:00 A.M., or even earlier. Since students, like everyone, need adequate sleep in order to learn well, an 11:00 P.M. curfew would help students to succeed in school."

While you may disagree with the conclusion of the above argument, you have to admit that there is a cause-and-effect connection between the evidence presented and the position that the author takes.

Unsafe Assumptions

There are two components to an argument: evidence and conclusion.

Evidence leads to conclusions. You need at least two pieces of evidence to support one conclusion. So, if you only give one piece of evidence, you must be making an assumption. Logic professors refer to assumptions as "suppressed premises,"

> **Steve Says:**
>
> Avoid being too familiar, colloquial, or humorous in your response to the prompt. Keep the reader interested, but make sure that the overall tone of the essay is formal.

which is just a fancy way to say, "unstated evidence." If you leave too much of your evidence unstated, your argument starts to get weak.

For example, if an essay says, "Curfews are dangerous because what if I have to be somewhere after 11:00?" The reader immediately starts to wonder, "Where could you have to be? What will you be doing?" There are simply too many unanswered questions. If you happen to agree with the position that the writer is taking, you tend to "help" with the assumptions and provide your own examples and answers to the unanswered questions. You might read the statement above and fill in an example from your own life or one that you would consider plausible. The graders at ACT will not do that extra thinking work for you as they read your essay. You have to be aware of the completeness of your essay and try to minimize the unanswered questions.

Too Conversational

This essay is supposed to be an example of your command of Standard Written English. The fact is that we often let each other "get away with" language in conversation that is simply not correct for Standard Written English. For example, if a friend uses *ain't* or *ya'll* in conversation, we would rarely correct him or her. Similarly, we all tend to use the term *you* when we really are speaking of people in general or people in a certain position, and not referring specifically to the reader or listener.

For example: "*You* could feel the tension in the room when Jeff had a pizza delivered to American History class." The person making that statement should have said, "*I* could feel the tension. . ." or "*We could all* feel the tension."

In general, you should try to leave *you* and *me* out of your essays. It is acceptable to use a personal example and refer to yourself (using "I") once or twice. However, some students get carried away and make the whole essay about themselves. The topics are meant to be relevant to high school students in general and usually refer to a policy matter. The stimulus is not an invitation to write a brief autobiography.

In conversation we often try to be inclusive and gender-neutral. The goal of including everyone is an ideal that this author shares. However, English forces us to use a gender-specific pronoun such as *he* or *she* or *him* or *her*. In conversation, we often ignore the incongruity when someone says, "Whoever forgot *their* umbrella is going to be sorry." The statement should be, "Whoever forgot *his or her* umbrella is going to be sorry."

One way to be inclusive is to alternate between male and female pronouns throughout your piece. This method can create some confusion for your reader. Another method is to use a plural phrasing rather than a singular phrasing: "*Those* who forgot *their umbrellas* are going to be sorry."

The overall thing to keep in mind is that your essay needs to be a formal document. It is not appropriate to write in the same idiom that you use with friends in informal conversation.

ESSAY SCORING

The ACT graders use a scoring *rubric* when they assign scores to essays. Basically, a rubric is a checklist of characteristics that the grader is supposed to look for when reading your essay. If your essay is more like the one described in the rubric as being a 5 than a 4, the grader will assign your essay a 5. The rubrics are posted on the ACT Web site and listed in ACT publications.

Since everyone knows what is expected, and there is virtually no chance that the grader will know the person who wrote a given essay, the system is reasonably fair. The graders are allowed to give a 6 to an essay that is somewhat less than perfect. The graders know that you have limited time to write, that you are doing this after you have just taken what may be the toughest exam of your life up to now, and that your fatigue and stress levels are likely to be elevated as a result.

Additionally, neatness is not specifically mentioned. However, the colleges to which you are applying will have access to your essay. This means that the people who are deciding on your applications may take your neatness into account. It also may have an impact on the graders as they assign a score to your essay. Since the scale runs from 1 through 6, there are some fine distinctions between say, a 4 and a 5. That difference could be important to the admissions personnel whom you are trying to impress. Nevertheless, the rubric descriptions of these two scores are very similar to each other. The difference between a 4 and a 5 could hinge on how the grader interprets words like *well-developed* (5) and *adequate* (4) or, what exactly makes an error "distracting."

So, make it easy on your grader to interpret those differences in your favor. Keep your essay neat and your handwriting legible. Nothing in the rules prevents you from printing rather than writing in cursive. So, if your printing will be easier for graders and admissions officials to read than your cursive, then by all means print.

Refer to the ACT website for a detailed description of the entire rubric and how each point level is described. In general, a 1 or a 2 usually indicates to graders and colleges that the person who wrote the essay either did not put forth a reasonable effort or is probably incapable of handling even basic college writing tasks. A 3 or 4 score means that the grader sees some fairly solid basic skills, but that there is plenty of room for improvement, and a 5 or 6 means that the author appears to be ready for challenging college-level work.

Keep in mind that the scores that are assigned by the graders are based on the essay only. The graders do not get to see your ACT multiple-choice scores. They just assign a point value to the essay and move on to the next one. They are not making comments on your worth as a human being or even your intelligence or ability. They are just giving feedback regarding how the essay stacks up to the rubric.

Colleges are likely to make use of the scoring information in different ways. You should do thorough research of the colleges to which you are applying to find out how they interpret ACT results.

SIMPLIFIED ESSAY SCORING RUBRIC

While each of the domains is scored on a scale of 2–12, that score reflects the total of two graders who each score on a scale of 1–6. So, in the following rubric, 6 is the best score available from an individual grader.

Score of 6: Demonstrates Effective Skill

Ideas and Analysis—Critically discusses multiple perspectives. Displays subtlety and precision. Provides context and discusses underlying assumptions.
Development and Support—Integrates skillful reasoning and illustration.
Organization—Unified in purpose and focus. Effectively uses transitions.
Language Use—Skillful and precise word choice. Sentences varied and clear. Effective voice and tone. Any minor errors in grammar, usage, or mechanics do not impair understanding.

Score of 5: Demonstrates Well-Developed Skill

Ideas and Analysis—Productively engages multiple perspectives. Addresses complexities and underlying assumptions.
Development and Support—Mostly integrated, purposeful reasoning and illustration. Capable.
Organization—Mostly controlled by unifying idea. Logical sequencing. Consistent transitions.
Language Use—Precise word choice. Mostly varied sentence structure. Any minor errors in grammar, usage, or mechanics do not impair understanding.

Score of 4: Demonstrates Adequate Skill

Ideas and Analysis—Engages multiple perspectives. Clear in purpose. Analysis recognizes complexity and underlying assumptions.
Development and Support—Clear reasoning and illustration.
Organization—Clear structure. Ideas logically grouped and sequenced. Transitions clarify relationships between ideas.
Language Use—Conveys clarity. Adequate word choice, sometimes precise. Clear sentences with some variety in structure. Appropriate style choices. Errors rarely impede understanding.

Score of 3: Demonstrates Some Developing Skill

Ideas and Analysis—Responds to multiple perspectives. Some clarity of purpose. Limited or tangential context. Somewhat simplistic or unclear.
Development and Support—Mostly relevant, but overly general or simplistic. Reasoning and illustration somewhat repetitious or imprecise.
Organization—Exhibits basic structure. Most ideas logically grouped. Transitions sometimes clarify relationships between ideas.
Language Use—Basic and only somewhat clear. Word choice occasionally imprecise. Little variety in sentence structure. Style and tone not always appropriate. Distracting errors that do not impede understanding.

Score of 2: Demonstrates Weak or Inconsistent Skill

Ideas and Analysis—Weak response to multiple perspectives. Thesis, if any, shows little clarity. Incomplete analysis.
Development and Support—Weak, confused, disjointed. Inadequate reasoning (circular, illogical, unclear).
Organization—Rudimentary structure. Inconsistent and unclear. Misleading transitions.
Language Use—Inconsistent, unclear, imprecise. Sentence structure sometimes unclear. Voice and tone inconsistent and inappropriate. Distracting errors sometimes impede understanding.

Score of 1: Demonstrates Little or No Skill

Ideas and Analysis—Fails to generate an intelligible argument. Unclear or irrelevant attempts at analysis.
Development and Support—Claims lack support. Reasoning and illustration are unclear, irrelevant, or absent.
Organization—Structure lacking. Transitions, if any, fail to connect ideas.
Language Use—Word choice imprecise, incomprehensible. Sentence structure unclear. Errors are pervasive and often impede understanding.

SAMPLE STUDENT RESPONSES

The following is a Sample Writing Prompt and examples of essays representing certain levels of the Scoring Rubric. We have also included an analysis of the scores assigned.

Violence in Video Games

Many people debate whether video game makers should be required to limit the violent content included in their products. There is concern over whether exposure to violence causes violent behavior. Given the prevalence and reach of video games and societal concerns about violent behavior in the real world, it is worth considering the implications of such a requirement.

PERSPECTIVE ONE	PERSPECTIVE TWO	PERSPECTIVE THREE
Human beings are creatures of habit. Exposing one's mind to intense, repeated simulated violence creates a stronger likelihood of actual violence. Desensitization through immersion in lifelike virtual worlds makes actual violence more acceptable to game players.	Game players are well aware that they are merely simulating violence. Violent play was common long before video games were invented. Gamers and their families should be free to decide what is appropriate for them.	All people should be free to decide what media they are exposed to. Attempts to limit access to information tread on the liberty of individuals to make their own choices. Censorship of video games is a dangerous threat to intellectual self-determination.

Essay Task

Write a unified, coherent essay in which you evaluate multiple perspectives on the implications of violence in video games and the suggestion to limit such violence. In your essay, be sure to:

- analyze and evaluate the perspectives given
- state and develop your own perspective on the issue
- explain the relationship between your perspective and those given

Your perspective may be in full agreement with any of the others, in partial agreement, or wholly different. Whatever the case, support your ideas with logical reasoning and detailed, persuasive examples.

Sample Essay—Score of 2

Products with violence shouldn't be limited. Nobody who play games get violent.

If there a choice to play violence games, than you should have it. Its not right to limit information or liberty, being that game players can decide what to play. So what if they make a habit of it. None of my friends are violent and we all play video games.

There is a difference between the real world and the world of video games. And most people know this, like my friends and classmates. We play video games all the time and the violence they say happens because of it is not something we do and I think people will agree with me.

In conclusion, don't limit products with violence. It doesn't work.

Score Analysis:

While the essay writer presents a clear thesis, the argument is not well developed and lacks an appropriate context. There is little support for the writer's position, and the writer fails to provide adequate examples in support of the position. The organization is clear but highly predictable, and it lacks cohesiveness and clear reasoning. The introduction and conclusion are not fully developed. Language is simple and at times inappropriate, with little variation in word choice. While sentence length is somewhat varied, there are too many distracting errors in grammar, usage, and mechanics.

Sample Essay—Score of 4

There is a lot of violence in the world. Some people think it might be caused by exposure to violent video games. I, for one, do not believe that. This is because, even though many people play violent video games for recreation, people know the difference between the real world and video games.

Many kids my age play violent video games, among others. We need something to take our minds off of school and work. My friends who are gamers are not violent as a result of playing video games. In fact, sometimes they play games so much that they are tired and distracted both in and out of school. In my opinion, a person who is tired tends to be non-violent. Also, my friends know the difference between real life and simulated violence, so they don't become desensitized to violence in the real world.

Furthermore, even people who are exposed to simulated violence don't become violent. For example, I see a lot of violence on TV and I play violent video games. Like my friends, this is somewhat a habit, but we are not violent. In fact, violent play was common long before video games were invented. People should be free do decide if they play violent video games or not. If you think that you will lose your freedom of decision, like some people think, then you should not be censored. Censorship can be a threat to freedom, so even if some people become violent by playing violent games, they should still be able to make a choice about playing the games. Limiting the violence in video games will not make an already violent person less violent.

In conclusion, video games should not be required to limit the violent content because we don't become violent just by playing video games. We know the difference between reality and video games, and should be able to make our own choices about whether or not we play a certain kind of video game.

Score Analysis:

The essay writer generates an argument that incorporates multiple perspectives on the given issue. The argument's thesis has a clear purpose and provides a relevant context for analysis of the issue and its perspectives. Development of ideas is mostly specific and logical, with some elaboration. Clear reasoning and examples adequately convey the significance of the argument. The organization of the essay is clear, though predictable. Ideas are presented in a logical sequence, but simple and obvious transitions are used. The introduction and conclusion are clear and generally well developed. Language is competent, with somewhat varied word choice and sentence length. Voice and tone are appropriate. There are a few errors in grammar, usage, and mechanics, but they are not distracting.

Sample Essay—Score of 6

Violence in video games is only one aspect of the larger topic of censorship. There is a concern that the nature of video games is sufficiently different from other media that censorship may be necessary to avoid horrifying real-world violence. Furthermore, since so many who play video games are children and young adults, censorship may be justified considering the impact on their developing brains.

One argument for censorship of video games focuses on the idea of desensitization. The theory seems to be that players are more likely to act upon violent impulses in their real lives after they've been exposed to the simulated violence of the virtual world. However, video games are played by many millions of people of all ages who do not act violently in their daily lives. We all know many people who play video games often. If video games caused violent behavior, we would all be aware of some of them who have committed real violent acts. That does not seem to be the case. I have friends who spend much of their spare time playing violent video games that simulate combat in vivid detail. Not only have I never felt threatened by them, I find them to be warm and caring people in their real lives.

It is important to remember that human beings have been violent since the beginning. A great deal of history consists of the study of war. Weapons have been on the forefront of technological development from the early days civilization up until today. Video games, on the other hand, are a relatively recent development. While it may be true that some gamers have been violent, it strains logic to say that playing video games causes violent behavior. Jack the Ripper is just one example of a person who committed terrible, violent crimes long before the advent of video games. Unless research shows a stronger connection between game play and actual violence beyond mere correlation, it does not seem that censorship is justified.

A very serious concern is the restraint of freedom that comes from all censorship. It is argued that each of us should be free to make our own decisions about the information we expose ourselves to. There have been calls for censorship as each new technology has come along. Our Constitution guarantees freedom of the "press" and, over time, the meaning of "press" has been expanded to include movies, sound recordings, and television, including violent content. Even comic books were censored in their early days. But, eventually, liberty won out and now consumers are free to expose themselves to violent content in all these media. There is no obvious reason to make a special exception for video games.

After considering all the perspectives, my own experiences, and my own knowledge, I am most convinced by Perspectives Two and Three. I stand on the side of liberty and do not believe that video games should be censored. However, I do believe that consumers should be given enough information to make up their own minds before they purchase and play video games. It would not be appropriate to market a game for young children that is described as safe for kids and then includes explicit, violent content. So, I can see the benefit of truth in advertising rules that force video game makers to be honest about the content of their games, even though I believe strongly in freedom of expression. As Perspective Two says, "Gamers and their families should be free to decide what is appropriate for them."

Score Analysis:

This essay makes an argument that critically engages with multiple perspectives on the issue. The author is opposed to censorship, but in favor of truthful descriptions of content. The essay discusses each of the perspectives given in the prompt. The argument employs insightful context and examines implications, complexities, and underlying values and assumptions. The author brings in the idea of "truth in advertising" and the protection of young children. The author links the discussion to the broader topic of censorship and discusses constitutional free speech values. The ideas are developed and follow an integrated line of reasoning. After a short introduction, each perspective is discussed and the ideas are deepened and broadened. Transitions between and within paragraphs strengthen the relationships among ideas. There are very few errors in grammar, usage, and mechanics. Word choice is skillful and precise.

SAMPLE ESSAY TO SCORE

Now that you've had a chance to learn about how the ACT essay is scored, read the following student essay written on the same prompt and generate a score for it. Follow the scoring guidelines on pages 31-32 to decide how you can make the essay better.

As our technology becomes more advanced, more and more teenagers take advantage of it. Playing video games has become increasingly prevalent. Recently, playing violent video games have sparked controversy regarding whether simulated violence is a direct causation of violence in the real world. While many video games do portray realistic scenes of bloodshed, I believe that people are aware of the differences between the virtual world vs the physical world.

While the increase in violent video games has a direct correlation to the increase in crime rates, correlation should not be mistaken for causation. Most people, while playing video games, are able to distinguish the difference between game and reality. This allows them to act logically and not act violently in real life as they would do in a video game. My cousin constantly plays Call of Duty, which is an extremely violent computer game. However, he has never acted violently against anyone even though he is always immersed in a game focused on killing.

Furthermore, video games should be encouraged among teens as it provides an accessible platform to hone their problem solving skills. Many video games such as soccer and basketball related ones don't include any violence at all. Instead, these games allow teens to learn essential skills such as teamwork and patience that are applicable in the real world. According to a friend, simulating soccer scenarios in video games not only allows him to improve his own technique, but also builds his confidence and character. Sometimes, movies and tv news display acts of violence far more gruesome than the ones seen in video games. Also, the bloodshed portrayed in some historical films is far more disturbing than the violence I've witnessed in video games.

In conclusion, with the increase in violence in video games and the controversy surrounding them, many people overlook the benefits brought on by video games. Therefore, I believe that content in video games should not be limited, because playing video games does not cause violence in the real world.

PART II

ACT Practice Test

This simulated tests should help you to evaluate your progress in preparing for the ACT. Take the test under realistic conditions (preferably early in the morning in a quiet location). Each of the test sections should be taken in the time indicated at the beginning of the sections. Fill in the bubbles on your answer sheet once you have made your selections.

When you have finished the test, check your answers against the Answer Key. Then, read the Explanations, paying close attention to the explanations for the questions that you missed.

ACT PRACTICE TEST
Answer Sheet

ENGLISH

1 Ⓐ Ⓑ Ⓒ Ⓓ	21 Ⓐ Ⓑ Ⓒ Ⓓ	41 Ⓐ Ⓑ Ⓒ Ⓓ	61 Ⓐ Ⓑ Ⓒ Ⓓ
2 Ⓕ Ⓖ Ⓗ Ⓙ	22 Ⓕ Ⓖ Ⓗ Ⓙ	42 Ⓕ Ⓖ Ⓗ Ⓙ	62 Ⓕ Ⓖ Ⓗ Ⓙ
3 Ⓐ Ⓑ Ⓒ Ⓓ	23 Ⓐ Ⓑ Ⓒ Ⓓ	43 Ⓐ Ⓑ Ⓒ Ⓓ	63 Ⓐ Ⓑ Ⓒ Ⓓ
4 Ⓕ Ⓖ Ⓗ Ⓙ	24 Ⓕ Ⓖ Ⓗ Ⓙ	44 Ⓕ Ⓖ Ⓗ Ⓙ	64 Ⓕ Ⓖ Ⓗ Ⓙ
5 Ⓐ Ⓑ Ⓒ Ⓓ	25 Ⓐ Ⓑ Ⓒ Ⓓ	45 Ⓐ Ⓑ Ⓒ Ⓓ	65 Ⓐ Ⓑ Ⓒ Ⓓ
6 Ⓕ Ⓖ Ⓗ Ⓙ	26 Ⓕ Ⓖ Ⓗ Ⓙ	46 Ⓕ Ⓖ Ⓗ Ⓙ	66 Ⓕ Ⓖ Ⓗ Ⓙ
7 Ⓐ Ⓑ Ⓒ Ⓓ	27 Ⓐ Ⓑ Ⓒ Ⓓ	47 Ⓐ Ⓑ Ⓒ Ⓓ	67 Ⓐ Ⓑ Ⓒ Ⓓ
8 Ⓕ Ⓖ Ⓗ Ⓙ	28 Ⓕ Ⓖ Ⓗ Ⓙ	48 Ⓕ Ⓖ Ⓗ Ⓙ	68 Ⓕ Ⓖ Ⓗ Ⓙ
9 Ⓐ Ⓑ Ⓒ Ⓓ	29 Ⓐ Ⓑ Ⓒ Ⓓ	49 Ⓐ Ⓑ Ⓒ Ⓓ	69 Ⓐ Ⓑ Ⓒ Ⓓ
10 Ⓕ Ⓖ Ⓗ Ⓙ	30 Ⓕ Ⓖ Ⓗ Ⓙ	50 Ⓕ Ⓖ Ⓗ Ⓙ	70 Ⓕ Ⓖ Ⓗ Ⓙ
11 Ⓐ Ⓑ Ⓒ Ⓓ	31 Ⓐ Ⓑ Ⓒ Ⓓ	51 Ⓐ Ⓑ Ⓒ Ⓓ	71 Ⓐ Ⓑ Ⓒ Ⓓ
12 Ⓕ Ⓖ Ⓗ Ⓙ	32 Ⓕ Ⓖ Ⓗ Ⓙ	52 Ⓕ Ⓖ Ⓗ Ⓙ	72 Ⓕ Ⓖ Ⓗ Ⓙ
13 Ⓐ Ⓑ Ⓒ Ⓓ	33 Ⓐ Ⓑ Ⓒ Ⓓ	53 Ⓐ Ⓑ Ⓒ Ⓓ	73 Ⓐ Ⓑ Ⓒ Ⓓ
14 Ⓕ Ⓖ Ⓗ Ⓙ	34 Ⓕ Ⓖ Ⓗ Ⓙ	54 Ⓕ Ⓖ Ⓗ Ⓙ	74 Ⓕ Ⓖ Ⓗ Ⓙ
15 Ⓐ Ⓑ Ⓒ Ⓓ	35 Ⓐ Ⓑ Ⓒ Ⓓ	55 Ⓐ Ⓑ Ⓒ Ⓓ	75 Ⓐ Ⓑ Ⓒ Ⓓ
16 Ⓕ Ⓖ Ⓗ Ⓙ	36 Ⓕ Ⓖ Ⓗ Ⓙ	56 Ⓕ Ⓖ Ⓗ Ⓙ	
17 Ⓐ Ⓑ Ⓒ Ⓓ	37 Ⓐ Ⓑ Ⓒ Ⓓ	57 Ⓐ Ⓑ Ⓒ Ⓓ	
18 Ⓕ Ⓖ Ⓗ Ⓙ	38 Ⓕ Ⓖ Ⓗ Ⓙ	58 Ⓕ Ⓖ Ⓗ Ⓙ	
19 Ⓐ Ⓑ Ⓒ Ⓓ	39 Ⓐ Ⓑ Ⓒ Ⓓ	59 Ⓐ Ⓑ Ⓒ Ⓓ	
20 Ⓕ Ⓖ Ⓗ Ⓙ	40 Ⓕ Ⓖ Ⓗ Ⓙ	60 Ⓕ Ⓖ Ⓗ Ⓙ	

READING

1 Ⓐ Ⓑ Ⓒ Ⓓ	11 Ⓐ Ⓑ Ⓒ Ⓓ	21 Ⓐ Ⓑ Ⓒ Ⓓ	31 Ⓐ Ⓑ Ⓒ Ⓓ
2 Ⓕ Ⓖ Ⓗ Ⓙ	12 Ⓕ Ⓖ Ⓗ Ⓙ	22 Ⓕ Ⓖ Ⓗ Ⓙ	32 Ⓕ Ⓖ Ⓗ Ⓙ
3 Ⓐ Ⓑ Ⓒ Ⓓ	13 Ⓐ Ⓑ Ⓒ Ⓓ	23 Ⓐ Ⓑ Ⓒ Ⓓ	33 Ⓐ Ⓑ Ⓒ Ⓓ
4 Ⓕ Ⓖ Ⓗ Ⓙ	14 Ⓕ Ⓖ Ⓗ Ⓙ	24 Ⓕ Ⓖ Ⓗ Ⓙ	34 Ⓕ Ⓖ Ⓗ Ⓙ
5 Ⓐ Ⓑ Ⓒ Ⓓ	15 Ⓐ Ⓑ Ⓒ Ⓓ	25 Ⓐ Ⓑ Ⓒ Ⓓ	35 Ⓐ Ⓑ Ⓒ Ⓓ
6 Ⓕ Ⓖ Ⓗ Ⓙ	16 Ⓕ Ⓖ Ⓗ Ⓙ	26 Ⓕ Ⓖ Ⓗ Ⓙ	36 Ⓕ Ⓖ Ⓗ Ⓙ
7 Ⓐ Ⓑ Ⓒ Ⓓ	17 Ⓐ Ⓑ Ⓒ Ⓓ	27 Ⓐ Ⓑ Ⓒ Ⓓ	37 Ⓐ Ⓑ Ⓒ Ⓓ
8 Ⓕ Ⓖ Ⓗ Ⓙ	18 Ⓕ Ⓖ Ⓗ Ⓙ	28 Ⓕ Ⓖ Ⓗ Ⓙ	38 Ⓕ Ⓖ Ⓗ Ⓙ
9 Ⓐ Ⓑ Ⓒ Ⓓ	19 Ⓐ Ⓑ Ⓒ Ⓓ	29 Ⓐ Ⓑ Ⓒ Ⓓ	39 Ⓐ Ⓑ Ⓒ Ⓓ
10 Ⓕ Ⓖ Ⓗ Ⓙ	20 Ⓕ Ⓖ Ⓗ Ⓙ	30 Ⓕ Ⓖ Ⓗ Ⓙ	40 Ⓕ Ⓖ Ⓗ Ⓙ

You may wish to remove these sample answer document pages to respond to the practice ACT Writing Test.

Begin WRITING TEST here.

Cut Here

If you need more space, please continue on the next page.

1

WRITING TEST

_____
_____
_____
_____
_____
_____
_____
_____
_____
_____
_____
_____
_____
_____
_____
_____
_____
_____
_____
_____
_____
_____
_____
_____
_____
_____

If you need more space, please continue on the back of this page.

Cut Here

WRITING TEST

_____

_____

_____

_____

_____

_____

_____

_____

_____

_____

_____

_____

_____

_____

_____

_____

_____

_____

_____

_____

_____

_____

_____

_____

_____

_____

_____

_____

_____

If you need more space, please continue on the next page.

3

Cut Here

WRITING TEST

_____

_____

_____

_____

_____

_____

_____

_____

_____

_____

_____

_____

_____

_____

_____

_____

_____

_____

_____

_____

_____

_____

_____

_____

_____

END OF THE WRITING TEST.
STOP! IF YOU HAVE TIME LEFT OVER, CHECK YOUR WORK ON THIS SECTION ONLY.

4

Cut Here

1 ■ ■ ■ ■ ■ ■ ■ ■ 1

ENGLISH TEST

45 Minutes – 75 Questions

DIRECTIONS: In the passages that follow, some words and phrases are underlined and numbered. In the answer column, you will find alternatives for the words and phrases that are underlined. Choose the alternative that you think is best and fill in the corresponding bubble on your answer sheet. If you think that the original version is best, choose "NO CHANGE," which will always be either answer choice A or F. You will also find questions about a particular section of the passage, or about the entire passage. These questions will be identified by either an underlined portion or by a number in a box. Look for the answer that clearly expresses the idea, is consistent with the style and tone of the passage, and makes the correct use of standard written English. Read the passage through once before answering the questions. For some questions, you should read beyond the indicated portion before you answer.

PASSAGE I

> The following paragraphs may or may not be in the most logical order. You may be asked questions about the logical order of the paragraphs, as well as where to place sentences logically within any given paragraph.

Noh Theater

[1]

Noh is a highly ritualized form of drama that <u>originate in</u> Medieval Japan as a type of play performed in front of nobility. Noh theater reached its apex in the fourteenth and fifteenth centuries with the works of a <u>playwright named Kannami and his son Zeami,</u> and it <u>is remaining largely unchanging.</u>

[2]

There are certain traits that make Noh unique in the Japanese theatrical world. The stage is always sparse, <u>only decorated solely</u> with a painting of a pine tree as a backdrop. Props are minimal and often symbolic. <u>The fan for example is a staple of Noh theater,</u> and it usually symbolizes another object. The costumes are

1. A. NO CHANGE
   B. original to
   C. originating in
   D. originated in

2. F. NO CHANGE
   G. playwright, named Kannami, and his son, Zeami,
   H. playwright named Kannami and his son Zeami;
   J. playwright named Kannami; and his son Zeami,

3. A. NO CHANGE
   B. has remained largely unchanged.
   C. will remain unchanging.
   D. will largely remain unchanged.

4. F. NO CHANGE
   G. decorated solely
   H. just decorated solely
   J. decorated only solely

5. A. NO CHANGE
   B. The fan, for example, is a staple of Noh theater,
   C. The fan for example, is a staple of Noh theater,
   D. The fan, for example is a staple, of Noh theater,

GO ON TO THE NEXT PAGE.

1 ■ ■ ■ ■ ■ ■ ■ ■ **1**

lavish and colorful, and the colors of the costumes are also symbolic. There is a chorus that often narrates, along with instrumentalists who add to the ambience with the unique and otherworldly music it plays.
6

[3]

7 If the audience is familiar with Noh, it can

recognize the characters among the stylized masks that
8
the actors wear. Certain masks represent certain types of characters and are intended to show specific traits possessed by these characters. The masks are intentionally painted in such a way that the different angles actually look like different facial expressions. 9

[4]

Noh theater combines poetry, dance, and music;
10

and often deals with supernatural themes. It is a very
10

sophisticated and subtle form of drama, and according to

legend, possesses something called *yugen*. An approximate

English translation of this abstract concept refers to
11

mystery and to what lies beneath the surface.

6. **F.** NO CHANGE.
   G. they play for.
   H. they play.
   J. it will play.

7. Which of the following sentences (assuming all are true) if added here, would best introduce the new subject of Paragraph 3?
   A. In the early days, Noh theater was sponsored by the elite rulers of Japan.
   B. Japanese theater has been popular for centuries.
   C. Masks also play an important role in Noh theater.
   D. There are archetypal characters who show up repeatedly in the repertoire of plays.

8. **F.** NO CHANGE
   G. with
   H. by
   J. for

9. At this point, the writer would like to highlight a very special talent that Noh actors must develop in order to be convincing. Which of the following sentences (assuming all are true) if added here, would most successfully achieve this effect?
   A. The actors wearing them must be skilled at tilting their heads in order to express nuances in emotion.
   B. The masks the actors wear are colorful and detailed and truly works of art.
   C. The actors must learn to express themselves in ways that are often unfamiliar to viewers of Western theater.
   D. Noh actors begin training at a very young age, so by the time they are much older, they have become very accomplished in their trade.

10. **F.** NO CHANGE
    G. Noh theater combines poetry dance and, music, and often deals with supernatural themes.
    H. Noh theater combines poetry, dance and music— and often deals with supernatural themes.
    J. Noh theater combines poetry, dance, and music, and often deals with supernatural themes.

11. Which of the following alternatives for the underlined portion would be LEAST acceptable?
    A. complex
    B. theoretical
    C. representational
    D. summarized

GO ON TO THE NEXT PAGE.

1 ■ ■ ■ ■ ■ ■ ■ ■ 1

[5]

[1] Most of the plays being performed today are the originals written by Kannami and Zeami, although a few new ones <u>had been written</u> since then. [2] Noh is not the most
12

popular form of theater in Japan today, <u>but it's</u> performers
13
are extremely dedicated, and people still buy tickets to enjoy this classic art form. [3] The fact that it has remained essentially in its original form for over 600 years <u>speak</u> to
14
its incredible beauty, mystique, and lasting elegance.

12. F. NO CHANGE
   G. will have been written
   H. have been wrote
   J. have been written

13. A. NO CHANGE
   B. also its
   C. but its
   D. because it's

14. F. NO CHANGE
   G. will speak
   H. speaks
   J. spoken

Question 15 asks about the preceding passage as a whole.

15. In reviewing her notes, the writer discovers that the following information has been left out of the essay:

> Zeami also wrote a treatise on the methodology of Noh, which is still studied by Noh actors.

If added to the essay, the sentence would most logically be placed after Sentence:
   A. 2 in Paragraph 2.
   B. 1 in Paragraph 5.
   C. 2 in Paragraph 3.
   D. 3 in Paragraph 5.

PASSAGE II

Calligraphy: Beautiful Writing

[1]

Art takes many forms, including watercolor painting, pencil sketching, <u>photography or sculpture.</u> One
16
lesser known and perhaps less appreciated art form is calligraphy, the elegant script of letters and figures.

16. F. NO CHANGE
   G. photography, sculpture.
   H. photography and to sculpture.
   J. photography, and sculpture.

GO ON TO THE NEXT PAGE.

1 ■ ■ ■ ■ ■ ■ ■ ■ 1

Many modern-day computer fonts are attempts to replicate this ancient art. [17]

The word *calligraphy* is derived from the Greek words
                              18
kalli, which means "beautiful," and *graphia*, which means "writing." It is difficult to say from which civilization
                                          19
calligraphy directly emerged, as many ancient peoples
          19
relied upon the written word and had some form of written records. Since the printing press wasn't invented until the mid-fifteenth century, legible handwriting was an important and useful skill throughout the known world.
                                    20

Chinese calligraphy date back to nearly 5,000 years.
                     21
Around 200 B.C., a 3,000-character index was established for use of Chinese scholars. These scribes
     22
having quickly developed their own styles
     23
when replicating the characters by varying the
              24
thickness of the lines, the amount of ink, and the types of paper. However, true "artists of script"
                  25

17. The writer is considering adding the following true statement after the preceding sentence:

   Computer fonts, however, cannot fully replicate the artistry and talent of an accomplished calligrapher.

   Would this be a relevant addition to the paragraph?
   A. Yes, because the writer goes on to discuss how calligraphy is an art form.
   B. Yes, because the passage continues to make references to modern technology.
   C. No, because the writer is focusing on calligraphy itself, not on specific calligraphers.
   D. No, because computer fonts have nothing to do with the art of calligraphy.

18. F. NO CHANGE
    G. derived with
    H. derived by
    J. derived to

19. A. NO CHANGE
    B. It is with difficulty that it is said which civilization calligraphy emerges from,
    C. From which civilization calligraphy directly emerged is difficult to say,
    D. Which civilization, it is difficult to say, from which calligraphy directly emerged,

20. F. NO CHANGE
    G. about
    H. from
    J. beside

21. A. NO CHANGE
    B. dated back to
    C. dates back
    D. dating back

22. F. NO CHANGE
    G. for use in
    H. for use with
    J. for use by

23. A. NO CHANGE
    B. quickly developing
    C. quickly developed
    D. who have quickly developed

24. F. NO CHANGE
    G. a lot of the characters
    H. the multitude of characters
    J. DELETE the underlined portion

25. A. NO CHANGE
    B. Soon,
    C. Yet,
    D. Otherwise,

GO ON TO THE NEXT PAGE.

1 ■ ■ ■ ■ ■ ■ ■ ■ **1**

emerged in Japan and <u>adapted</u> Chinese calligraphy around
                  26

the seventh century, developing their own style, which

included an appreciation <u>for</u> imperfection as well as
                          27

technical ability.

     In Europe, <u>calligraphy was greatly influencing by the</u>
                                28

<u>development of the Church</u> during the Middle Ages.
           28

Manual recording and duplication of religious texts

demanded an abundance of beautiful handwriting.

A variety of styles soon emerged, including Gothic

calligraphy. In the Gothic style, letters are <u>more spaced close,</u>
                                  29

and lines are much narrower than in other styles.

Because the print takes up less space, less paper

is required.

     Today, calligraphy continues to fascinate both scribes

and art aficionados alike. Modern calligraphy equipment,

such as specialized pens, inks, and paper, <u>makes</u> the art
                                    30

fairly easy to learn.

26. **F.** NO CHANGE
    G. adapts
    H. adapting
    J. having adapted

27. **A.** NO CHANGE
    B. with
    C. to
    D. unto

28. **F.** NO CHANGE
    G. the development of calligraphy greatly influenced by the Church
    H. the Church greatly influenced the development of calligraphy
    J. calligraphy greatly influenced by the development of the Church

29. **A.** NO CHANGE
    B. close and spaced
    C. more closely spaced
    D. spaced closely

30. **F.** NO CHANGE
    G. making
    H. make
    J. made by

PASSAGE III

Early American Fur Trappers

     The myth of the early American mountain men <u>paints</u>
                                         31

a picture of romance, adventure, and intrigue. In reality,

most mountain men were fur traders <u>acting to participate</u>
                                      32

in a tough business that sent them for months at

a time to the vast rivers and mountains of the American

West. For the most part, beaver pelts were the primary

target of these unconventional businessmen, as beaver

31. **A.** NO CHANGE
    B. paint
    C. by painting
    D. painting

32. **F.** NO CHANGE
    G. participating
    H. who, acting to participate
    J. choosing to act and participate

GO ON TO THE NEXT PAGE.

1 ■ ■ ■ ■ ■ ■ ■ ■ **1**

hats and coats were all the rage in early American towns and cities. 33

While some fur trappers and traders traveled alone, many worked together in groups for a particular trading company. The Hudson Bay Company, well-known throughout Europe,

was the world's first and largest fur-trading company. Its
_____
34

buyers would rendezvous at designated sites in America
_____
35
where trappers presented furs in exchange for money or

essential goods. 36

While the mountain man appear to personify "rugged
_____
37
individualism," he was completely dependent upon his

ability to trap wild animals and, therefore, relied upon

consumer demand in those pelts.
_____
38

33. At this point, the writer is considering adding the following sentence:

> While not inexpensive, harvesting beaver pelts directly from North America was far cheaper than importing them from across the ocean.

Would this be a relevant addition to make here?
A. Yes, because the writer needs to establish that beaver pelts were very expensive.
B. Yes, because the sentence emphasizes the importance of the American mountain man's contribution.
C. No, because the paragraph focuses on the American mountain man, not on beaver pelts.
D. No, because beaver pelts from other countries cost more than those obtained in America.

34. F. NO CHANGE
    G. first and, largest
    H. first and largest;
    J. first, and, largest

35. A. NO CHANGE
    B. designating
    C. designate
    D. and designate

36. Given that all of the following sentences are true, which one should be placed here to offer a logical explanation for why trappers sometimes traded their furs for goods instead of money?
    F. While mountain men were skilled hunters and could capture their own food, they still needed many supplies in order to survive.
    G. Many Indian tribes were willing to trade goods and supplies with the mountain men.
    H. Some mountain men had families back in the cities and towns, so money was important.
    J. Trappers enjoyed trading goods and supplies among themselves, as long as the Hudson Bay Company approved.

37. A. NO CHANGE
    B. appeared to
    C. appear
    D. appears to

38. F. NO CHANGE
    G. by
    H. with
    J. for

GO ON TO THE NEXT PAGE.

1 ■ ■ ■ ■ ■ ■ ■ ■ 1

While some of the trappers were <u>employing</u> a particular
                                    39
fur company, others chose to be freelancers.

Men <u>hired directly, by a fur company</u> were called
            40
"engagers," and all furs they obtained were

company property <u>and not for personal use.</u>
                        41

The "free-trapper" was the most autonomous of <u>all; he</u>
                                                      42
trapped wherever and with whomever he chose. He also

traded or sold his furs at his own discretion. Although the

free-trappers were considered by their peers to be tough

and hardy <u>because of</u> their ability to endure the hardships
            43
of mountain living, many of these mountain men

eventually <u>succumb</u> to those hardships.
              44

39. **A.** NO CHANGE
    B. under the employment of
    C. employed by
    D. DELETE the underlined portion.

40. **F.** NO CHANGE
    G. hired directly, by a fur company
    H. hired directly by a fur company
    J. hired, directly by a fur company

41. **A.** NO CHANGE
    B. that were given directly to the company
    C. and did not belong to them
    D. DELETE the underlined portion.

42. **F.** NO CHANGE
    G. all:
    H. all, he
    J. all he

43. **A.** NO CHANGE
    B. in regards with
    C. because
    D. irregardless of

44. **F.** NO CHANGE
    G. succumbing
    H. will be succumbing
    J. succumbed

Question 45 asks about the preceding passage as a whole.

45. Suppose the writer had intended to write an essay that
    explored the myth of the American mountain man.
    Would this essay successfully fulfill the writer's goal?
    A. No, because the essay focuses on American myths
        in general, not just the myth of the American
        mountain man.
    B. No, because American mountain men did not actu-
        ally exist.
    C. Yes, because the writer explains how the American
        mountain man story is really a myth.
    D. Yes, because the writer discusses the contrast
        between the romantic, mythical side of the moun-
        tain man's life and the reality of his job.

GO ON TO THE NEXT PAGE.

1 ■ ■ ■ ■ ■ ■ ■ ■ 1

PASSAGE IV

The Green Bay Packers

In 1919, Curly Lambeau returned home to Green Bay, Wisconsin to playing football at Notre Dame from a severe case of tonsillitis. In a conversation with his friend George Calhoun, he expressed regret at not being able to play football since returning home. Calhoun decides to recommend that Curly start a team in his home town. Excited by the idea, Lambeau convinced his boss at the Indian Packing Company to donate uniforms and the use of an athletic field.

Curly ran ads in the local newspaper, inviting other athletes to join the new team. Only 20 football players joined the team the first year. Although Lambeau named the team the Big Bay Blues, fans and players called the team the Packers.

The conditions under which the Packers played during that first year were a far cry from those enjoyed by modern present - day football teams. They played their games in an empty field behind Hagemeister Brewery. There were no locker rooms, so players normally changed into their uniforms at home before the game. There were no gates or bleachers; so there was no way to charge admission or accurately count attendance.

46. **F.** NO CHANGE
 G. from playing football at Notre Dame, due to a severe case of tonsillitis.
 H. from a case of severe tonsillitis, which was due to playing football at Notre Dame.
 J. from playing football at Notre Dame, which was due to a severe case of tonsillitis.

47. **A.** NO CHANGE
 B. recommended to him a decision
 C. recommended
 D. gives his recommendation

48. **F.** NO CHANGE
 G. the Packers, they were called by the fans and players of the team.
 H. the team was called the Packers by the fans and the players.
 J. the fans called the team the Packers, the players, too.

49. **A.** NO CHANGE
 B. contemporary
 C. up-to-date
 D. DELETE the underlined portion

50. **F.** NO CHANGE
 G. before the game into their uniforms at home.
 H. uniforms at their home before the game.
 J. into their uniforms, which were at home before the game.

51. **A.** NO CHANGE
 B. gates or bleachers, so there was no way to charge admission
 C. gates, or bleachers, so there was no way to charge admission
 D. gates or bleachers. So there was no way to charge admission

GO ON TO THE NEXT PAGE.

Without fences and stands, the only way <u>by raising</u> money
⁵²

<u>was quite literally to pass</u> a hat around to spectators for
⁵³

donations. 54

In 1920, bleachers were built on one side of
Hagemeister Park, located behind the brewery. The largest
recorded attendance at that location was 6,000 fans for the
game against the Minneapolis Marines on October 23, 1921.

That was the Packers' first official game <u>that was played</u>
⁵⁵
as part of the new American Professional Football
Association, which is now known as the National
Football League. 56

From their humble beginnings, the Packers have gone
on to win more NFL championships than any other team,
including four Super Bowls. The Packers now play in a

newly renovated stadium <u>being named</u>
⁵⁷

Lambeau Field <u>after the legendary status of the</u>
⁵⁸
<u>team's founder.</u> The stadium now seats 72,515—and
⁵⁸
over 60,000 people are on the waiting list for season
tickets! The team has come a long

52. F. NO CHANGE
   G. it raised
   H. to raise
   J. they could raise any

53. A. NO CHANGE
   B. was, quite literally to pass,
   C. was quite literally, to pass
   D. was, quite literally, to pass

54. The writer is considering changing the first sentence of
this paragraph (assuming that if there is an error, it has
been fixed). Which sentence would be the best choice?
   F. The writer should not replace the sentence.
   G. The Packers endured brutal conditions in the first
year, all for the love of the game.
   H. When the Packers played their first season, professional football was not very popular nationwide.
   J. Equipped with a popular new name, the Packers
were ready to begin their first season.

55. A. NO CHANGE
   B. they played
   C. for playing
   D. DELETE the underlined portion

56. The writer would like to link the information already
presented about the Green Bay Packers to the information in this paragraph. Assuming all are true, which of
the following sentences best achieves this effect?
   F. Vince Lombardi coached the Packers with great
success in the 1960s.
   G. The Packers are the only publicly owned team in
the NFL.
   H. In the 1950s, Curly Lambeau was fired by the Packers as part of an internal power struggle.
   J. This historic game marked the beginning of the
Green Bay Packers, one of the oldest franchises in
professional football.

57. A. NO CHANGE
   B. named after
   C. named
   D. naming

58. F. NO CHANGE
   G. after the team's legendary founder.
   H. after the legend of the team's founder.
   J. after the team founder's legendary status.

GO ON TO THE NEXT PAGE.

1 ■ ■ ■ ■ ■ ■ ■ **1**

way from wearing donated uniforms and passing
₅₉
a hat around a nearly empty field.
₅₉

59. A. NO CHANGE
   B. way, from wearing donated uniforms, and passing a hat around a nearly empty field.
   C. way from wearing donated uniforms; and passing a hat around a nearly empty field.
   D. way from wearing donated uniforms and passing a hat around, a nearly empty field.

> Question 60 asks about the preceding passage as a whole.

60. Suppose the writer had been assigned to write a brief essay illustrating the economic influence of the Packers on the city of Green Bay. Would this essay fulfill that assignment?
   F. Yes, because the essay indicates that the team relied on a corporate sponsorship to get started.
   G. Yes, because the essay indicates that the team has been very successful.
   H. No, because the essay primarily focuses on how the team was started and its eventual success.
   J. No, because the essay notes that the team relied on donations rather than charging admission.

PASSAGE V

Prepare for the Starfish Inn

"Are we really planning on staying here?" Sophie asked me incredulously. "I feel like we have no choice!" I responded. The place in question was the Starfish Inn, a motel of dubious character on the beach in Jacksonville, Florida. We ended up here largely of our own
₆₁
irresponsibility. It was our freshman year of college, yet yearning to escape the cold and dreary weather for
₆₂
the sun of spring break, we decided to head south. It was a last-minute decision; we did not make reservations anywhere.

When we arrived in Florida, we tried to book a room in a decent, affordable hotel. After visiting six hotels and finding no vacancy, we stopped at an information booth. A
₆₃
kind and helpful woman delivered the discouraging news

61. A. NO CHANGE
   B. instead of
   C. because of
   D. in part of

62. F. NO CHANGE
   G. and
   H. but
   J. where

63. A. NO CHANGE
   B. were stopped by
   C. had to stop for
   D. stopping at

GO ON TO THE NEXT PAGE.

1 ■ ■ ■ ■ ■ ■ ■ ■ 1

that, if we didn't have reservations anywhere, it would be very difficult for us to possess lodging. She recommended

        64

that we check a couple of places, but they all seemed far beyond our limited

budget, which was small Then she said that the Starfish

        65

Inn was reasonably priced, but that she would not want

her daughters to stay there!

    So there's how we got into our predicament. After

       66

paying the proprietor of the motel, we dragged our

luggage to the room, where we opened the door with

         67

great trepidation. The room was a starfish-themed

nightmare! Everything was in shades of blue, green,

and turquoise, with real and depicted starfish on nearly

every surface; so the place looked like it hadn't been

                     68

redecorated since 1975!

   68

    [1] With grim determining, we shuffled across the

           69

somewhat gritty floor to further check out the place. [2] The

couch was threadbare and lumpy and not exactly inviting.

[3] The television was equipped with a rusty, flimsy, antenna

                        70

that reminded me of the television that my grandpa

kept in his basement workshop. [4] On the down side,

71

however, the small kitchen table was so rickety that I was

afraid to actually use it. [5] On the plus side, the room

did have a kitchenette, so we could save money by

cooking some meals inside. 72

    Confronted with all of these problems, Sophie and I

decided we had one option—to make the best of it and

---

64. Which choice provides the most appropriate image?
- F. NO CHANGE
- G. secure
- H. capture
- J. grab

65. A. NO CHANGE
- B. budget.
- C. budget. Our budget was pretty typical for college students.
- D. budget. I wanted to have enough money left to buy souvenirs.

66. F. NO CHANGE
- G. it's
- H. that's
- J. its

67. A. NO CHANGE
- B. so
- C. we
- D. DELETE the underlined portion.

68. F. NO CHANGE
- G. surface, the place looked like it hadn't been redecorated since 1975!
- H. surface (looking like it hadn't been redecorated since 1975).
- J. surface; the place looked like it hadn't been redecorated since 1975!

69. A. NO CHANGE
- B. determined
- C. determination
- D. determine

70. F. NO CHANGE
- G. with a rusty, flimsy antenna
- H. with a rusty flimsy, antenna
- J. with a rusty flimsy antenna

71. A. NO CHANGE
- B. will keep
- C. in keeping
- D. keep

72. For the sake of unity and coherence, Sentence 5 of this paragraph should be placed:
- F. where it is now.
- G. immediately before Sentence 2.
- H. immediately before Sentence 3.
- J. immediately before Sentence 4.

GO ON TO THE NEXT PAGE.

1 ■ ■ ■ ■ ■ ■ ■ **1**

enjoy ourselves! We thought that it was about time to escape the pseudo-undersea atmosphere of the room and enjoy some real ocean views. 73

73. The writer would like to conclude the final paragraph with a sentence that shows the shift in attitude she and her friend Sophie experienced. Which choice would best accomplish this?
   A. I begrudgingly accepted the fact that our motel room was terrible as we headed to the beach.
   B. As the old saying goes: "When life gives you lemons, make lemonade."
   C. We headed to the beach moaning about our crazy motel room.
   D. I decided that my next spring break trip will definitely not be in Florida!

Questions 74 and 75 ask about the preceding passage as a whole.

74. The writer is considering the addition of the following sentence to the essay:

   I couldn't help but be reminded of one of the most fascinating facts about starfish: that if you chop one up, a new starfish will grow from each remaining stump.

   Given that this statement is true, should it be added to the essay, and if so, where?
   F. Yes, at the end of the second paragraph because the lady at the information booth mentioned the Starfish Inn. Adding the sentence would be an effective way for the writer to foreshadow the troubles she and her friend would soon have at the motel.
   G. Yes, at the end of the third paragraph, because the writer had just finished describing the starfish theme of the room.
   H. No, because it is evident that the writer is not interested in scientific facts.
   J. No, because a scientific statement would be out of context in an essay describing the personal experiences of the writer and her friend.

75. Suppose a travel agent hired the writer to write an article warning of the possible hazards of being unprepared for a vacation. Does this essay successfully fulfill the assignment?
   A. Yes, because the first paragraph clearly states that the writer and her friend traveled to Florida.
   B. Yes, because the essay gives an example of what can happen when you don't make reservations before going on vacation.
   C. No, because the essay is primarily intended to be a humorous story about being forced to stay at a dilapidated motel.
   D. No, because the essay concerns college students and does not consider that others may also be unprepared for a vacation.

END OF THE ENGLISH TEST.
STOP! IF YOU HAVE TIME LEFT OVER, CHECK YOUR WORK ON THIS SECTION ONLY.

3 ━━━━━━━━━━━━━━━━━━━━━━━━━━━━━━━━━━ **3**

READING TEST

35 Minutes – 40 Questions

DIRECTIONS: This test includes four passages, each followed by ten questions. Read the passages and choose the best answer to each question. After you have selected your answer, fill in the corresponding bubble on your answer sheet. You should refer to the passages as often as necessary when answering the questions.

PASSAGE I

PROSE FICTION: *Born in Paradise*

Martin spent most of his childhood in a tropical paradise on the island of Barbados. Despite the pleasant climate, Martin's early life was difficult. His father left when Martin was a baby, and his mother, Sheila, worked
5 long hours as a housekeeper at a nearby hotel. Martin was left to be cared for by his teenage brothers. In the best of times, the selfish boys let Martin fend for himself; in the worst of times, they made Martin the target of their pranks. Eventually, Martin's mother recognized
10 his plight and enlisted the help of Martin's grandmother.

Granny loved Martin dearly, but the elderly woman did not have the energy to keep up with a feisty toddler. As often as possible, she took Martin to the rundown neighborhood playground so that he could burn off
15 some of his excess energy. On the endless rainy days of summer, she was often heard to exclaim, "Oh, Martin! What am I gonna do with you?"

To help fill the long, muggy days, Granny began taking Martin to the island's library. There they sat for
20 hours as she slowly read him story after story. When her voice grew tired, young Martin would beg her to teach him to read. "Oh, Martin. You're too young to read, dear," she would reply. But Martin was determined, and his inquisitiveness prevailed. Soon, the symbols on the
25 page took on meaning; as the rainy season ended, Martin begged to continue their library excursions.

"Sheila, Martin is special."

Sheila absently looked up.

"What's that, Mom?"

30 "I said, 'Martin is special!'"

"Oh. Yeah. And, listen, I really appreciate you taking care of him like you have. In a couple of years he can go to school and then it will all be so much easier!"

"I'm not sure it will. When I said he was special
35 I didn't just say it because I'm his grandmother. He's special." She paused and then continued, "You know, he can read."

"It is wonderful the way he likes books and all."

"Have you ever let him read to you?"

40 "Of course! He comes into my room almost every morning and recites his favorite book. He even turns the pages. It's very cute!"

"Sheila! Pay attention! I know you're tired from working long hours, but Martin isn't reciting—he's
45 reading! In all my years I have never seen a four-year-old like him. By next month he'll be reading books that are beyond me!"

Sheila's mother continued: "Honey, the schools here will be too easy for Martin, and you can't afford
50 to send him to one of those fancy international schools. You have got to get to America where they'll have schools for a child like Martin."

"Mom, think what you're saying! I can't just pick up and move to another country! The older boys aren't even
55 finished with school yet, and there's no way they'd leave their friends! Besides, I can't possibly afford to move to America. Do you have any idea how much it costs to live there?"

"Slow down! I'm not telling you to leave today.
60 I'm telling you to start planning and saving. Your older boys will be done with school in a few years. Then they can fend for themselves. Oh, don't give me that look— I'll look after 'em! But you gotta start makin' plans for Martin. Honey, he doesn't like to be bored, and that's
65 gonna be a problem pretty soon. He's a good boy, and he'll behave in these schools while he's still young. But I can't promise that he'll be able to control himself when he realizes he knows more than the teachers! I don't want to see that precious baby wasting his life and get-
70 ting into trouble! Sweetie, he's got a gift, and you gotta do something with that gift."

Sheila paused for a long moment as she struggled to comprehend all that her mother was telling her. Finally, she sighed. "Okay."

75 "What's that?"

"I said, 'okay.' I trust you. I'll start finding out what I need to do to get Martin and me to America. But I don't know what we're gonna do when we get there!"

"Just work on getting there. You can figure out the
80 rest later."

GO ON TO THE NEXT PAGE.

3 ⬛⬛⬛⬛⬛⬛⬛⬛⬛⬛⬛⬛⬛⬛⬛⬛⬛⬛⬛⬛⬛⬛ **3**

1. When Granny says, "I'm not sure it will," (line 34) she is expressing her concern that:
   A. schools in Barbados are dangerous.
   B. Martin is hyperactive and will likely behave poorly in school.
   C. the school will not provide the academic challenge that Martin requires.
   D. life never gets any easier.

2. It can be reasonably inferred from their conversation that Granny believes Sheila is:
   F. not as well-educated as Martin is.
   G. too overworked to recognize Martin's gift.
   H. an incompetent parent.
   J. overly solicitous with her sons.

3. The idea that Martin's mother is unaware of his abilities is best exemplified by which of the following quotations from the passage?
   A. "He even turns the pages. It's very cute!"
   B. "Do you have any idea how much it costs to live there?"
   C. "Mom, think what you're saying!"
   D. "I really appreciate you taking care of him like you have."

4. As it is used in line 33, the word *it* most nearly refers to the:
   F. library excursions.
   G. reading of books.
   H. taking care of Martin.
   J. start of the school year.

5. It can be inferred from the passage that Granny is:
   A. Martin's paternal grandmother.
   B. Sheila's mother-in-law.
   C. Martin's maternal grandmother.
   D. an unknown wealthy benefactor.

6. The passage makes it clear that Martin and his mother:
   F. plan to move to America.
   G. do not get along.
   H. will be alienated from Martin's brothers.
   J. will never see Granny again.

7. You may reasonably infer from the details in the passage that Sheila is:
   A. self-confident.
   B. never going to make friends in America.
   C. negligent in her care of her older sons.
   D. willing to do whatever it takes to help Martin succeed.

8. You may reasonably infer from the passage that Martin's brothers:
   F. attended a school for juvenile delinquents.
   G. often read books to Martin.
   H. were not well-liked in school.
   J. cared more for themselves than for Martin.

9. Within the passage, the main function of the second paragraph is to:
   A. describe the special bond between a grandmother and grandson.
   B. explain the deplorable living conditions of the main characters.
   C. provide evidence of a potential conflict in the story.
   D. introduce a comparison between an old woman and a young child.

10. The title, "Born in Paradise," combined with details presented in the passage implies that:
    F. everyone loves a tropical island.
    G. only natives can attend school in Barbados.
    H. American schools are inferior.
    J. paradise is a relative term.

GO ON TO THE NEXT PAGE.

3 ████████████████████████████████████ **3**

PASSAGE II

SOCIAL SCIENCE: The following passages discuss different battles of the Civil War.

Passage A

The bloodiest single day of war in United States history came when General Robert E. Lee's Confederate Army undertook its first engagement on Northern soil. According to the Antietam National Battlefield, when
5 the fighting had subsided, more than 23,000 soldiers lay dead or wounded, more than all of the dead or wounded Americans in the Revolutionary War, War of 1812, Mexican War, and Spanish-American War combined.

Just a week after his army's victory in the Second
10 Battle of Bull Run, Lee resolved to advance the front into Northern territory. The vast farm fields of western Maryland were ready for harvest, and Lee saw in them an opportunity to nourish his soldiers, replenish his supplies, and turn the residents of the undecided border state to his cause.

15 So with great fanfare, Lee and fellow General "Stonewall" Jackson marched their ragged Army of Northern Virginia across the Potomac River and straight through the Frederick town square. Lee issued the *Proclamation to the People of Maryland* to invite the citizens
20 to join the Southern movement. Soldiers obeyed Lee's order to refrain from violence and pillaging, so for several days the townspeople maintained tacit compliance and sold food, clothes, and shoes to Southern troops. Lee keenly observed, however, that while pleasant, the
25 people of Maryland reserved no sympathy for the Confederate side, so he needed a revised plan.

Forces would divide to take western Maryland and then reform to advance along the railroad toward Harrisburg, Pennsylvania, a crucial Union transport hub.
30 General Jackson led 22,000 troops southwest to Harpers Ferry to engage the 12,000-man Federal fortification. Lee's remaining 18,000 soldiers would march over the mountains 25 miles to Hagerstown and wait for the others. On September 10, 1862, all began their march. No one
35 knew how fateful it would be.

Lee soon realized that the Union was a step ahead. Its Army of the Potomac was reassembled in days instead of the weeks Lee had forecast. In addition, the Harpers Ferry garrison had remained instead of fleeing as Lee had
40 imagined it would upon learning of his advance. Lastly, an enlisted man searching a recently abandoned Confederate camp had recovered a copy of Lee's order detailing the siege of Maryland.

Union General George McClellan moved his forces west through Frederick, and Lee caught word
45 of it. Knowing the peril his divided troops were in, he ordered men to fortify the paths across the mountains, granting sufficient time to the majority of his soldiers to establish a defensive position near Sharpsburg. Simultaneously, McClellan and his 85,000 men waited along
50 Antietam Creek outside town. By nightfall on September 16, the stage was set for the devastating Battle of Antietam, which would begin at sunrise.

Passage B

The three days of the Battle of Gettysburg, Pennsylvania, constitute the bloodiest fight of the Civil War—50,000 combatants falling dead or wounded or disappearing.
55 Gettysburg is often cited as the last crucial battle of the war before the Confederate surrender. In the intervening two years, the Confederate Army would never again attempt such a grand offensive in the North. On the last day of battle, Union forces
60 anticipated and defused what is now known as Pickett's Charge, the final assault ordered by General Robert E. Lee, leaving Confederate forces in tatters.

Lee approached the third day of Gettysburg with the same strategy as he had the day before. He would divide his forces to attack Federal positions from both
65 the east and the west. Troops under General James Longstreet were to take up the assault on Culp's Hill. However, standing by at dawn, Longstreet and his men unexpectedly suffered a devastating artillery bombardment from Union troops intent on reclaiming the previous day's losses.

70 Lee hastened to revise his plan of attack. Nine brigades were set to attack Federal positions in the center of the line on Cemetery Ridge. The selection of troops for this mission was the first of many Confederate blunders that doomed Pickett's Charge. Confederate
75 General A. P. Hill was ill, so responsibility for his men was passed to General George Pickett, who failed to distinguish between Hill's well-rested men and those who had recently fought in battle. Indeed the battle-fatigued soldiers that made the charge fell into ranks in a thicket behind the cannons.

80 Longstreet initiated the infantry assault under orders from General Lee. The Southern force numbered over 12,000 men across nine brigades to form a mile-long offensive front. The thousand-yard march to within musket range of the Union fortifications was peppered
85 with harrowing artillery fire. When cannonade became fusillade, the mile of men had narrowed to nearly half. Flanking fire from the left decimated an entire brigade. Forces in the center wheeled to support them but were met with a musket attack from the Eighth Ohio Infantry
90 regiment, which had unexpectedly moved to ambush the Confederate soldiers. The Virginians under General Pickett brought up the rear and retook the fight to the left. Soon, their right flank was exposed to calamitous enfilade fire from the Vermont Brigade. Remaining
95 Confederates succeeded in a partial breech of the center Union line, but reinforcements from the right quickly put down the Southern offensive.

The charge was a massacre. Pickett's brigade commanders, each of his 13 regiment leaders, and nearly half his 12,000 enlisted men fell during the assault. Union
100 dead or wounded numbered fewer than 2,000. Today at Gettysburg, a monument commemorates the "high water mark" of the Confederacy along Cemetery Ridge, for after Pickett's Charge on July 3, 1863, the Army of the South never fully recovered and began the series of
105 retreats and surrenders that concluded the Civil War.

GO ON TO THE NEXT PAGE.

3 ■■■■■■■■■■■■■■■■■■■■■ **3**

Questions 11 – 13 ask about Passage A.

11. As it is used in line 3, the word "engagement" most nearly means:
    A. match.
    B. commitment.
    C. arrangement.
    D. confrontation.

12. In line 15 the phrase "so with great fanfare" suggests that General Lee was:
    F. broken and despondent.
    G. fatigued from recent battle.
    H. eager to promote his cause.
    J. satisfied with his army's progress.

13. Which statement about the Army of Northern Virginia, if true, would most directly support the view described in lines 20–23?
    A. General Lee was a powerful but often barbaric man.
    B. Soldiers were difficult to control in times of great stress.
    C. Soldiers took great pains to keep their uniforms and equipment tidy.
    D. A rigid chain of command maintained strict order throughout the ranks.

Questions 14 – 17 ask about Passage B.

14. As it is used in line 58, "grand" most nearly means:
    F. haughty.
    G. massive.
    H. wonderful.
    J. extravagant.

15. According to Passage B, Pickett's Charge failed because of which of the following?
    I.   Artillery fire
    II. Infantry charges
    III. Exhausted soldiers
    A. I only
    B. II only
    C. I and II
    D. I, II, and III

16. It can reasonably be inferred from Passage B that the statement "the mile of men had narrowed to nearly half" (line 86) suggests that the Confederate line:
    F. moved within firearms range.
    G. was suffering massive losses.
    H. was easy for Union soldiers to target.
    J. made very slow progress across the field.

17. In lines 101–102, the quotation marks around the phrase "high water mark" serve to:
    A. indicate that this word is used allegorically.
    B. emphasize the limitations of military conquest.
    C. criticize the human preoccupation with expansion.
    D. emphasize the uniqueness of the author's writing.

Questions 18 – 20 ask about both passages.

18. Unlike the author of Passage A, the author of Passage B does which of the following?
    F. Details a specific battle.
    G. Explains a war strategy.
    H. Questions an officer's decision.
    J. Offers an alternative interpretation.

19. Both Passage A and Passage B indicate that the Civil War:
    A. was amicably resolved.
    B. denied certain freedoms to Americans.
    C. resulted in many casualties on both sides.
    D. decided the borders of all fifty states in the Union.

20. Which of the following most accurately describes a way in which the two passages are related to each other?
    F. Passage A introduces a topic that is further detailed in Passage B.
    G. Passage B suggests an alternate framework within which to interpret Passage A.
    H. The history suggested in Passage A is proven to be false by the facts in Passage B.
    J. The evidence presented in Passage B serves to weaken the assertions made in Passage A.

GO ON TO THE NEXT PAGE.

3   **3**

PASSAGE III

HUMANITIES: *The Passion of Perugino*

I remember feeling slightly disconcerted as I looked up at the unsmiling saints, the Virgin Mary, and even Jesus as I wandered through the hushed halls of the museum. The unworldly experience continues to haunt my mem-
5 ory as I recall the unflinching gazes of Pietro Perugino's subjects staring blankly at me as I admired the power and beauty of the great Italian Renaissance master's most famous works of art. For years, I had studied great artists of the past and present, but not even the breath-
10 taking landscapes of Monet could prepare me for the moment that I was confronted with the genius of one of the least well known artists of the Italian Renaissance. In that moment, my admiration for artists like Renoir and Manet of the French Impressionist Movement, was
15 eclipsed by the austere exquisiteness of these fifteenth-century paintings.

Since that day in the museum, I have gained more knowledge and expertise about the Italian Renaissance movement, and I recognize that Pietro Perugino's work is not beyond critique. His paintings have been
20 described as monotonous and unimaginative because the people portrayed often look alike without any distinguishing features. His paintings lack the ingenuity and fluidity of Sandro Botticelli. Perugino's own pupil, Raphael, could surpass his teacher in creating emotion on the canvas. The genius Michelangelo could evoke
25 dreaminess in his work that creates a feast for the imagination, while keeping minuscule details in perfect perspective. And yet, Pietro Perugino's paintings are still the ones that I see in my mind when I hear the words *Italian Renaissance*.

30 I remember being awestruck as I viewed his fresco *The Delivery of the Keys* (1482) and noticing the elegant simplicity of the painting, which portrayed St. Peter accepting the keys to heaven. The painting should have paled next to the other more dramatic work in the Sis-
35 tine Chapel, but *The Delivery of the Keys* held its own with its voluminous clouds and elegant gothic buildings in the background. In this piece, Pietro Perugino showed how far art had come since the medieval times. Instead of flat and cardboard-like characters, the sub-
40 jects in *The Delivery of the Keys* display awe, disbelief, and amazement while engrossed in conversation with each other. Perugino also experimented with depth, and he rivaled Leonardo da Vinci in his ability to create a definite background and foreground. *The Deliv-
45 ery of the Keys* boasts a gorgeous mountain landscape that truly appears to be miles away from St. Peter as he accepts the key to eternity.

During our tour of the Sistine Chapel, the guide had shared with us the story of Perugino's life. Perugino would almost starve to death because he forgot to eat or sleep
50 while painting. Rest was never an option for this driven artist. His dedication shined through in his meticulous, yet

passionate work. The love that Perugino had for painting shows in the careful detail of works like *The Delivery of the Keys*. In my mind, Perugino's passion for art gives his
55 pieces their distinction and this passion more than makes up for any deficiencies that his critics might find.

I have seen the works of several painters from the Italian Renaissance that are considered far greater than anything created by Perugino. Paintings by
60 Michelangelo, Leonardo da Vinci, and Botticelli are certainly more in demand and enjoy mainstream popularity and acceptance. All of these three artists seemed capable of creating more dramatic and majestic pieces than did Perugino. The work of da Vinci and Michelangelo is seen on postcards and reprinted
65 on cheap posters everywhere because of its universal appeal. Although the brilliance of all of the Italian Renaissance masters is undeniable, the awe-inspiring beauty of Michelangelo's work or the subtle detail of da Vinci's *Mona Lisa* cannot match the simple passion
70 evident in Perugino's paintings. In spite of being more simple and less appealing to the masses, Perugino's paintings reveal raw talent and skill that I have never seen equaled by another artist anywhere in the world.

21. Which of the following descriptions most accurately and completely represents this passage?
    A. A reminiscent and passionate recollection of the narrator's introduction to Perugino's art
    B. An independent critical analysis of Monet, Renoir, and Manet in relation to Perugino
    C. An impartial evaluation of the paintings of Perugino
    D. A thorough biographical outline of Perugino's life

22. All of the following were unmistakably identified as painters in this passage EXCEPT:
    F. Leonardo da Vinci.
    G. Michelangelo.
    H. Botticelli.
    J. Donatello.

23. Which of the following quotations best expresses the main point of the passage?
    A. "Since that day in the museum, I have gained more knowledge and expertise about the Italian Renaissance movement, and I recognize that Pietro Perugino's work is not beyond critique."
    B. "I have seen the works of several painters from the Italian Renaissance that are considered far greater than anything created by Perugino."
    C. "In this piece, Pietro Perugino showed how far art had come since the medieval times."
    D. "In my mind, Perugino's passion for art gives his pieces their distinction and this passion more than makes up for any deficiencies that the critics might find."

GO ON TO THE NEXT PAGE.

3   **3**

24. As it is used in the passage (line 22), the word *ingenuity* most nearly means:
  F. resourcefulness.
  G. inventiveness.
  H. quality.
  J. versatility.

25. It can be inferred from the passage that the narrator most highly values which of the following in an artist?
  A. Fluidity and volatility
  B. Unique appearance of subjects
  C. Devotion and passion for art
  D. Classical training from the masters

26. It can be most reasonably concluded from the writer's quote, "In that moment, my admiration for artists like Renoir and Manet of the French Impressionist Movement, was eclipsed by the austere exquisiteness of these fifteenth-century paintings," (lines 12–15) that:
  F. few of the painters of the French Impressionist Movement were as talented as the artists of the Italian Renaissance.
  G. the masters of the Italian Renaissance are more universally accepted than Renoir and Manet.
  H. the narrator believes that the technical skill and creativity of Perugino surpasses that of Renoir and Manet.
  J. the narrator's admiration of Perugino is so great, he or she believes that Perugino's work outshines that of more well-known painters.

27. According to the passage, what are characteristics of Perugino's work?
  I. austerity
  II. showing the passion of the artist
  III. ability to display depth
  IV. abstraction
  A. I, II, III only
  B. I, II only
  C. I, IV only
  D. I, II, IV only

28. Which of the following best describes the narrator's instant reaction upon seeing Perugino's paintings for the first time?
  F. Disbelief in the quality of the work
  G. Unsettled by some of the features of the paintings
  H. Envious of Perugino's genius and artistic ability
  J. Intent on comparing Perugino's work to French Impressionist artists

29. All of the following are a criticism of Perugino's paintings mentioned in the passage EXCEPT:
  A. Perugino's paintings show a lack of imagination.
  B. Perugino's technique in creating depth was not as advanced as Leonardo da Vinci's.
  C. the subjects or people of Perugino's paintings often look alike.
  D. Raphael could create more emotion in his paintings than Perugino.

30. The narrator states his or her opinion about famous artists and their work throughout the passage. All of the following opinions are clearly stated in the passage EXCEPT:
  F. Manet's work is reprinted on postcards and cheap posters because of its popularity.
  G. Leonardo da Vinci and Perugino could both display depth well.
  H. Botticelli's work shows fluidity and ingenuity.
  J. the painting *Mona Lisa* by Leonardo da Vinci shows subtle detail.

GO ON TO THE NEXT PAGE.

3 ▬▬▬▬▬▬▬▬▬▬▬▬▬▬▬▬▬▬ **3**

PASSAGE IV

NATURAL SCIENCE: *The Prickly Porcupine*

As we timidly watched the lumbering escape efforts of this oversized rodent, we were struck by its own apparent lack of fear and panic. Then it dawned on us that, unlike most other animals in
5   the wild, the porcupine's mere outward appearance provides more than adequate reason for it rarely to become alarmed or excited. Even knowing that the "shooting-quills" forest legend really is just that, stumbling upon this threatening creature is sure to
10 cause fear and panic only from the human's point of view and not vice versa.

The *Erethizon dorsatum* (Latin for "irritable back") comes equipped with more than 30,000 quills on its back, sides, and tail. Each of these
15 quills contains several barbs, or hook-like structures, that can imbed themselves into the flesh of a predator. Rather than throwing their quills, however, porcupines are able to implant them into their would-be attacker when the animal or human gets
20 too close. Porcupines also swing their tails back and forth, slamming quills into their adversaries. Since these quills are hollow, they fill up with the host's blood once imbedded, making them even more difficult to remove. Many a dog has found itself with
25 a noseful or mouthful of porcupine quills, which need to be tended to right away. Often, clipping an inch or so off the end of the quills before removing them can aid in their extraction and relieve the excruciating pain.

30 The porcupine ranks second in size to the beaver among the rodent family. A full-grown porcupine can range anywhere from two to three and a half feet in length and generally weighs between eight and fourteen pounds. However, a porcupine with a plentiful food supply can weigh considerably
35 more. Female porcupines generally give birth once a year to a single offspring. The long, seven-month gestation period ensures a well-developed infant that is nearly ready at birth to take care of itself. Born with soft quills, it takes only a few hours after
40 birth for these quills to harden and be ready for an attack. There are some animals, however, that are able to break down the porcupine's powerful defense system by carefully turning the porcupine over onto its back, exposing its soft and vulnerable underbelly. Bobcats, cougars, and coyotes are
45 especially adept at this technique and pose a major threat to the porcupine.

Porcupines are mostly found in northern and cold climates. They are particularly fond of forested areas, as mature trees provide both food and shelter.

50 During the winter months, porcupines chew almost exclusively on tree bark. As nocturnal animals, porcupines generally sleep high up in a tree during the day, though they also use underground burrows, particularly in the spring while tending their newborns.

55 According to the Yukon Department of Environment, the porcupine has been useful to and appreciated by many. Quills are often used in jewelry- and basket-making, as well as in decorating clothing and shoes. Porcupine meat is even considered to be a tasty meal and fairly easy to obtain. In British Columbia, however,
60 the porcupine has developed a negative reputation due to its appetite for wood, damaging trees and even wooden buildings.

While porcupines can be a source of worry to some people, they are fascinating animals to observe.
65 Because of their incredible defense systems, they take their time to escape a potential enemy, which allows for a great opportunity to view these animals fairly closely. Just don't get too close!

31. The primary purpose of the passage is to:
   A. detail the various ways in which the quills of a porcupine are used by humans.
   B. give a brief overview of the porcupine, its habitat, and the misconceptions associated with it.
   C. prove false the "shooting-quills" legend associated with the porcupine.
   D. detail the safest way to remove porcupine quills from animals such as dogs and beavers.

32. The author calls the porcupine a "threatening creature" (line 9) in the first paragraph because:
   F. it is a timid creature.
   G. it is merely a forest legend.
   H. it becomes alarmed and excited.
   J. it has a frightening appearance.

33. The passage indicates that, unlike some other wild animals, the porcupine:
   A. has a descriptive scientific name.
   B. does not have a defense mechanism.
   C. is not easily frightened.
   D. generally finds plenty of food.

34. According to the author, the porcupine most likely moves slowly because:
   F. its quills add extra weight.
   G. it has no reason to move quickly.
   H. it has no predators.
   J. it has short legs.

GO ON TO THE NEXT PAGE.

3 ██ **3**

35. Based on information in the passage, the author feels dogs are especially threatened by porcupines because:
    A. dogs are larger than porcupines.
    B. dogs are likely to touch porcupines with their noses and mouths.
    C. porcupines only attack dogs.
    D. porcupines often wander into peoples' backyards.

36. The passage indicates that the Yukon government considers porcupines to be both:
    F. scarce and endangered.
    G. appreciated and useful.
    H. dangerous and unthreatening.
    J. feared and disliked.

37. Which of the following quotations best captures the second paragraph's (lines 12–28) main focus?
    A. "Each of these quills ... can imbed themselves into the flesh of a predator" (lines 14–16).
    B. "Rather than throwing their quills" (line 17).
    C. "Porcupines also swing their tails" (line 20).
    D. "Since these quills are hollow, they fill up with the host's blood" (lines 21–23).

38. The passage indicates that a porcupine turned over on its back would most likely be:
    F. safe to approach.
    G. killed by predators.
    H. unnoticed or ignored.
    J. ready to attack.

39. The passage indicates that, if imbedded, a porcupine's quills:
    A. can cause death.
    B. can be very painful.
    C. should be left alone.
    D. will eventually fall out on their own.

40. According to the passage, the scientific name for the porcupine means:
    F. "prickly animal."
    G. "shooting quills."
    H. "threatening creature."
    J. "irritable back."

END OF THE READING TEST.
STOP! IF YOU HAVE TIME LEFT OVER, CHECK YOUR WORK ON THIS SECTION ONLY.

WRITING TEST

DIRECTIONS: This test is designed to assess your writing skills. You have forty (40) minutes to plan and write an essay based on the stimulus provided. Be sure to take a position on the issue and support your position using logical reasoning and relevant examples. Organize your ideas in a focused and logical way, and use the English language to clearly and effectively express your position.

When you have finished writing, refer to the Scoring Rubrics discussed in Chapter 7 to estimate your score.

Note: On the actual ACT you will receive approximately 2.5 pages of scratch paper on which to develop your essay, and approximately 4 pages of notebook paper on which to write your essay. We recommend that you limit yourself to this number of pages when you write your practice essays.

Seat Belt Laws

Most states currently have laws on the books requiring some or all of the occupants of motor vehicles to fasten their seat belts while the vehicle is in motion. Penalties for operation of a motor vehicle while passengers are unrestrained range from simple fines to potential loss of driving privileges. In many states, there are exceptions for school buses and antique vehicles which were never equipped with seat belts. In some states, a vehicle may not be stopped by law enforcement merely for a seat belt violation, while in other states, officers may stop and ticket a driver for a seat belt violation alone.

PERSPECTIVE ONE	PERSPECTIVE TWO	PERSPECTIVE THREE
Seat belt laws save lives. The statistics show that occupants who are properly restrained are much more likely to survive a serious accident than those who are not. Traffic fatalities nationwide have decreased significantly over the past few decades as seat belt laws have been passed by state after state.	Seat belt laws are an infringement on our basic freedoms. Government does not have the right to force adult citizens to act responsibly simply for their own good. Each individual person is responsible for his or her own safety and society should not be permitted to penalize a person for taking a risk with his or her own body.	Society must bear the medical expenses due to increased injury to individuals who do not use seat belts. Car accidents are still common, even with modern antilock brakes and other similar technologies. In many cases, automobile insurance will not cover treatment for injuries attributable to failure to use safety equipment, leaving all of us to foot the bill.

Essay Task

Write a unified, coherent essay in which you evaluate multiple perspectives on the implications of seat belt laws. In your essay, be sure to:

- analyze and evaluate the perspectives given
- state and develop your own perspective on the issue
- explain the relationship between your perspective and those given

Your perspective may be in full agreement with any of the others, in partial agreement, or wholly different. Whatever the case, support your ideas with logical reasoning and detailed, persuasive examples.

ANSWER KEY

English Test			Reading Test	
1. D	26. F	51. B	1. C	21. A
2. F	27. A	52. H	2. G	22. J
3. B	28. H	53. D	3. A	23. D
4. G	29. C	54. F	4. H	24. G
5. B	30. F	55. D	5. C	25. C
6. H	31. A	56. J	6. F	26. J
7. C	32. G	57. C	7. D	27. A
8. H	33. C	58. G	8. J	28. G
9. A	34. F	59. A	9. C	29. B
10. J	35. A	60. H	10. J	30. F
11. D	36. F	61. C	11. D	31. B
12. J	37. B	62. G	12. H	32. J
13. C	38. J	63. A	13. D	33. C
14. H	39. C	64. G	14. G	34. G
15. B	40. H	65. B	15. D	35. B
16. J	41. D	66. H	16. G	36. G
17. A	42. F	67. A	17. A	37. A
18. F	43. A	68. J	18. F	38. G
19. A	44. J	69. C	19. C	39. B
20. F	45. D	70. G	20. F	40. J
21. C	46. G	71. A		
22. J	47. C	72. J		
23. C	48. F	73. B		
24. F	49. D	74. J		
25. B	50. F	75. C		

ANSWERS AND EXPLANATIONS

English Test Explanations

PASSAGE I

1. **The best answer is D.** The underlined portion must be a verb with tense, or else the sentence would be a fragment. Therefore, eliminate answer choices B and C. Answer choice D, which has past tense, is best because the sentence clearly states that Noh began in *Medieval Japan*, a past time period.

2. **The best answer is F.** This question requires you to select the correct punctuation for the underlined portion. Answer choice G has unnecessary commas. Both answer choice H and answer choice J improperly use semicolons. The comma after *Zeami* is necessary because the two independent clauses are conjoined with *and*.

3. **The best answer is B.** The sentence references a time period in the past (*fourteenth and fifteenth centuries*). To describe an action (in this case, staying unchanged) that began in the past and is ongoing in the present, the present perfect tense is appropriate. Only answer choice B uses this verb tense.

4. **The best answer is G.** The words *only*, *just*, and *solely* all have similar meaning. To avoid redundancy, you should use only one of them in the sentence. Eliminate answer choices F, H, and J.

5. **The best answer is B.** The interrupting phrase *for example* should always be set off by commas when it appears within a sentence. The only answer choice that places a comma before and after *for example* is answer choice B.

6. **The best answer is H.** The noun being replaced by the pronoun in this sentence is *instrumentalists*, which is plural. Therefore, you must use the plural pronoun *they*. Eliminate answer choices F and J. The noun *scores* is the direct object of the verb *play*, so no preposition (*for*) is necessary. Eliminate answer choice G.

7. **The best answer is C.** Paragraph 3 discusses the *stylized masks* worn by the actors to reflect certain characters. The sentence that best introduces this topic is answer choice C.

8. **The best answer is H.** The actors, not the characters that they portray, wear the masks, so you can eliminate answer choice F. The word *with* suggests that the audience is wearing the masks; eliminate answer choice G. In English idiom, someone *recognizes* something or someone *by* some feature or characteristic.

9. **The best answer is A.** This question requires you to select an answer choice that discusses a *unique talent*. Answer choice A explains that *tilting their heads* is a specific skill that must be learned, so it is the best selection. The other answer choices either are too general or they include information about the masks, not the actors.

10. **The best answer is J.** A semicolon must be immediately followed by an independent clause or a phrase that starts with a conjunctive adverb such as *therefore*. Eliminate answer choice F because the semicolon is not followed by an independent clause. The items in a list must be separated by commas if there are three or more items in the list. The only remaining choice with correct comma usage is answer choice J.

11. **The best answer is D.** In context, the adjective *abstract* means *nonspecific* or *somewhat difficult to define and understand*. While an *abstract* is a summary of a text, speech, and so on, this definition is not appropriate based on the context.

12. **The best answer is J.** The most important clue indicating the correct tense is the adverb *since*, which denotes a duration of time beginning in the past. Eliminate answer choice G because it refers to the future. In this case, the time period extends to the present. It did not end in the past, so the past perfect tense is not appropriate here. Eliminate answer choice F, which is a present perfect passive-voice construction. In passive constructions, as in H and J, the past participle is used. The past participle of *write* is *written*, not *wrote*, which is the simple past form. Eliminate answer choice H.

13. **The best answer is C.** First, decide whether you should use *its* or *it's*. In this sentence, the noun *Noh theater* is being replaced by the pronoun *it*. The *performers* belong to the theater, so you should use the possessive form of *it*, which is *its*. Eliminate answer choices A and D. There is a contrast suggested in the second half of the sentence, so the correct conjunction is *but*, making answer choice C correct.

14. **The best answer is H.** The *fact* mentioned in this sentence exists now. Second, the subject must agree with the verb. In this sentence, the subject is the long noun clause *the fact that it has remained essentially in its original form for over 600 years*. Although this noun clause ends with a plural noun, the central, controlling noun that determines its grammatical number is *fact*, which is singular. Therefore, a singular verb is needed, *speaks*, answer choice H.

15. **The best answer is B.** The sentence contains information on Zeami, one of the original playwrights. Zeami is not discussed in either Paragraph 2 or Paragraph 3, so eliminate answer choices A and C. Since you are left with Paragraph 5, decide whether the sentence should be placed after Sentence 1 or Sentence 3. As Sentence 1 mentions Zeami, it would make sense to place the new sentence after Sentence 1.

PASSAGE II

16. **The best answer is J.** The items in a series must be separated by commas. While answer choice G contains the correct number of commas, it omits the conjunction *and*, which is essential to the sentence.

17. **The best answer is A.** The preceding sentence mentions computer fonts. It is appropriate to provide a transition into the rest of the passage that is concerned with calligraphy as an art form.

18. **The best answer is F.** The verb *derive* (here as a past participle in a passive-voice construction) can take as a complement to a prepositional phrase beginning with *from*, in which case it means originate (*from...*). This subject of the sentence, *calligraphy*, has its origins in the two Greek words *kalli* and *graphia*.

19. **The best answer is A.** The sentence as it is written is clear and concise and in the active voice. The other answer choices are awkward.

20. **The best answer is F.** This question requires you to best express the idea that legible handwriting was important and useful in many places.

21. **The best answer is C.** The sentence is describing a general property (the age) of Chinese calligraphy. Therefore, the simple present tense is appropriate. The subject *Chinese calligraphy* is third-person, singular; therefore, the verb must be third-person, singular: *dates*, answer choice C.

22. **The best answer is J.** This is a passive-voice sentence in which *Chinese scholars* is the agent (who or what does the action of the verb). With active voice, *Chinese scholars* would be the subject. Recall that making sentences passive usually results in moving the subject to the end of the sentence and after the preposition *by*. This is the function of *by* required in this underlined portion. Eliminate answer choices F and H. Next, recognize that *for use by* is idiomatic, whereas *for the use by* is not. Therefore, answer choice J is best. If you cannot recognize that idiom, select answer choice J because it is more concise.

23. **The best answer is C.** According to the passage, the scribes started using the index around 200 B.C., which is clearly in the past. Therefore, you should use the simple past form of the verb *develop*.

24. **The best answer is F.** This question requires you to express the idea clearly and concisely. It is mentioned previously in the paragraph that the scribes replicate a 300-character index. Therefore, any reference to quantity is unnecessary.

25. **The best answer is B.** This question requires you to choose the best conjunctive adverb. A conjunctive adverb can be used to join two independent but related ideas, and is often used at the beginning of a sentence, if that sentence is related to the one directly preceding it. The conjunctive adverbs *however*, *yet*, and *otherwise* suggest a contrast that doesn't exist in this paragraph. It makes sense that soon after the scribes developed their own, individual styles, the scribes would emerge as artists.

26. **The best answer is F.** The subject of the sentence, true artists of script, "emerged" and "adapted."

27. **The best answer is A.** It is idiomatic in this context to say *appreciation for*.

28. **The best answer is H.** This question requires you to express the idea clearly and concisely. First, determine whether it is the *Church* or the *calligraphy* that is being influenced. Based on the context of the passage, it makes sense that the *calligraphy* is being influenced. Eliminate answer choices G and J, which suggest that *calligraphy* influenced the *Church*. It is better to use the active voice, as in answer choice H, which clearly indicates that the *Church* influenced *calligraphy*.

29. **The best answer is C.** To maintain parallelism within this sentence, the adjective phrase *closely spaced* must be in the comparative form (*more closely spaced*) to match the comparative form *narrower*.

30. **The best answer is F.** The singular subject *equipment* requires a singular verb. Remember that subject and verb must match in tense.

PASSAGE III

31. **The best answer is A.** The *myth* that is the subject of this sentence exists in the present, so the simple present tense is appropriate. Eliminate answer choices C and D. The *myth* is singular, so use the singular verb *paints*, answer choice A.

32. **The best answer is G.** To avoid redundancy, use only the verb *participating* in this sentence. The remaining answer choices are awkward and redundant.

33. The best answer is C. The primary focus of the first paragraph is the mountain man, not the beaver pelts that he harvested. Therefore, the sentence would not be a relevant addition to the paragraph. Answer choice D is not correct because the statement is off-topic.

34. The best answer is F. There is no punctuation required in this phrase that includes two adjectives describing the same noun.

35. The best answer is A. To maintain parallel construction in this sentence, match the verbs "designated" and "presented."

36. The best answer is F. It makes sense that the mountain men would need goods other than the food they captured. (They may have needed clothes, ammunition, cooking utensils, etc.) The other answer choices contain information that is outside the scope of the passage.

37. The best answer is B. It is important to maintain parallelism within the sentence. So, the subject and verb must have the same form. Since the subject, *mountain man*, is singular, the verb must also be singular. Eliminate answer choices A and C. The other verb forms in the sentence, *was* and *relied*, are past tense, so eliminate answer choice D, which includes the present-tense verb *appears*.

38. The best answer is J. This question requires you to recognize that *consumer* is used as the first noun of a compound with the noun *demand*. Any form of the verb *demand* would create an ungrammatical sentence. Therefore, answer choices F, G, and H can be eliminated.

39. The best answer is C. The logical opposite of *freelancers* is being an employee of a firm. Only answer choice C expresses that some trappers were employed by *a particular fur company*.

40. The best answer is H. With commas, provided that all grammar rules are followed, fewer is better. In this sentence, the passive voice verb construction were *called* has the noun phrase *Men hired directly by a fur company* as its subject. The noun *Men* is modified by the past participle phrase *hired directly by a fur company*, so no comma should separate them. Eliminate answer choices F, G, and J.

41. The best answer is D. The sentence already says that the furs were *company property*, so it is not necessary to include any more information about to whom the furs did or did not belong. Answer choices A, B, and C are all redundant and should be eliminated.

42. The best answer is F. A semicolon should be followed by an independent clause that provides more information about the first part of the

sentence. The sentence is correct as written. You should not use a comma to separate two main clauses. This is known as a comma splice. Eliminate answer choice H. It is necessary to include some form of punctuation, so eliminate answer choice J. By removing the word *he* in answer choice G, an incomplete sentence is created.

43. The best answer is A. The sentence structure suggests a cause-and-effect relationship. The phrase *because of* provides the proper connection between the effect and the cause. *Irregardless* is not a word and should never be used, so eliminate answer choice D.

44. The best answer is J. The paragraph is in the past tense, therefore it is appropriate to use the past tense verb *succumbed*. The sentence as it is written uses the present tense verb; answer choices G and J use the "-ing" form of the verb, which is incorrect in this context.

45. The best answer is D. This question requires you to determine the main idea of the essay. The essay introduces the concept of the myth of the mountain man, and then goes on to describe the reality of living as a mountain man, which was quite different. Answer choice D best supports the ideas presented in the essay.

PASSAGE IV

46. The best answer is G. It is idiomatic to return home *from* some place. Answer choice F says *from a severe case of tonsillitis*, so it can be eliminated. Answer choices H and J can be eliminated because the relative pronoun *which* and the verb *was* make them wordy. In addition, answer choices H and J attribute, respectively, the tonsillitis to playing football and playing football to the tonsillitis.

47. The best answer is C. It is important to maintain parallelism within the paragraph. The verbs *returned, expressed,* and *convinced* are all past tense. Therefore, a past-tense verb should be used in the underlined portion. Eliminate answer choices A and D. Eliminate answer choice B because it is awkward. The simplest way to express the idea conveyed in the sentence is to use *recommended*, answer choice C.

48. The best answer is F. This question requires you to express the idea clearly, concisely, and in the correct word order. First, determine who is the logical subject of the verb *called*. *Fans and players* had their own nickname for the team. Answer choice F is best because it has active voice. Answer choice H has passive voice, so it can be eliminated. Answer choice J is awkward; it, too, can be eliminated.

49. **The best answer is D.** The modifiers *present-day*, *contemporary*, and *up-to-date* all have the same meaning, so none of them can be the correct answer. Since the sentence already includes the word *modern*, it would be redundant to include any of the answer choices. Therefore, omit the underlined portion, answer choice D.

50. **The best answer is F.** This question requires you to express the idea clearly and concisely. Answer choice H suggests that they were already wearing uniforms and had to change into different uniforms at home. This is not supported by information in the paragraph, so eliminate answer choice H. Answer choice G separates the verb *changed* from its prepositional phrase complement *into their uniforms*, so it is somewhat awkward and can be eliminated. Answer choice J is wordy and can be eliminated.

51. **The best answer is B.** In this sentence, *so* is a coordinating conjunction joining two independent clauses. Independent clauses joined with coordinating conjunctions must be separated by a comma placed immediately before the conjunction. Eliminate answer choices A and D. When two nouns are joined with a coordinating conjunction (here, *gates* and *bleachers*), no comma should be used. Therefore, eliminate answer choice C.

52. **The best answer is H.** Idiomatically, the noun *way* can take a verb in the infinitive form (*to* + bare form) as a complement. In this case, that is the clearest and most concise way to express the intended idea.

53. **The best answer is D.** The phrase *quite literally* is an interrupting phrase; therefore, it should be set apart from the sentence using commas.

54. **The best answer is F.** The first sentence as it is written adequately introduces the main idea of the paragraph (the Packers' humble beginnings) and does not need to be replaced. While the conditions under which the Packers played football during the first year were difficult, the paragraph does not support the idea that the conditions were *brutal*, so eliminate answer choice G. The other answer choices are not supported by the context of the paragraph.

55. **The best answer is D.** By definition, a *game* is *played*; therefore, answer choices A, B, and C are redundant and can be eliminated.

56. **The best answer is J.** This question asks you to find a way to *link* information already given in the passage with the information that is to follow. Since the paragraph introduces the *historic game* played at Hagemeister Park and indicates that it was the first game that the Packers played as professionals,

answer choice J makes the most sense. The other answer choices refer specifically to individuals or contain irrelevant information.

57. **The best answer is C.** The adjective *named* is appropriate to precede a building's proper name, here *Lambeau Field*. Answer choice A can be eliminated for wordiness. Answer choices B and D are awkward structurally and logically and can be eliminated.

58. **The best answer is G.** According to the passage, Lambeau Field was *named after* a person named Lambeau. *Founder* in answer choice G correctly and succinctly refers to this man.

59. **The best answer is A.** The verb *come* takes a prepositional object beginning with *from* and is modified by the phrase *a long way*. Therefore, no commas are needed between any of these elements. Eliminate answer choice B. Answer choice C can be eliminated because a semicolon joins dependent clauses. The verb *pass* takes a prepositional indirect object (to whom or to what place the direct object passes). No comma must separate verb from object, so eliminate answer choice D.

60. **The best answer is H.** This question requires you to determine the main idea of the essay. The essay focuses primarily on the beginnings of the Green Bay Packers and some of the team's success and doesn't really have anything to do with any economic influence the team may have had on the city of Green Bay.

PASSAGE V

61. **The best answer is C.** The sentence following the sentence containing the underlined portion explains how the author and her friend ended up at the Starfish Inn. The conjunction *because of* implies that the reason they ended up at the Starfish Inn was their own irresponsibility. Answer choice C is the clearest choice.

62. **The best answer is G.** The coordinate conjunction *and* suggests that, in addition to it being their freshman year of college, the friends wanted to get away for spring break. *Yet* and *but* suggest a contrast that doesn't exist, so eliminate answer choices F and H. The word *where* suggests a specific location; freshman year of college is not a location, so eliminate answer choice J.

63. **The best answer is A.** To maintain parallelism in this paragraph, verbs must have the same form. *Arrived, tried, delivered*, and so on are past forms. Answer choice D has future tense, so eliminate it. Answer choice C is wordy and awkward, so eliminate it. Answer choice B uses the passive voice, and it is awkward in this sentence.

64. **The best answer is G.** The underlined portion should mean "obtain." This eliminates answer choice F. Answer choices H and J have similar meanings, but they are too literal to be used with *lodging*. Only answer choice G has the correct meaning and is appropriate to use with *lodging* or other services.

65. **The best answer is B.** The adjective *limited* modifying *budget* implies that the budget is small. Therefore, the sentence as written is redundant. Eliminate answer choice A. The second sentence in each of answer choices C and D is irrelevant to the topic of the passage, so they can be eliminated.

66. **The best answer is H.** It is idiomatic to use *that's* to refer to the implied reason the girls were in a predicament.

67. **The best answer is A.** The word *where* indicates a location. The girls dragged their luggage to the room (the location) and then opened the door. Answer choices B and D create incomplete sentences and should be eliminated. Answer choice C creates a comma splice, so it can be eliminated.

68. **The best answer is J.** This question requires you to select the correct punctuation, while maintaining the meaning of the sentence. A semicolon should be followed by an independent clause, which is the case in answer choice J. Since *The place looked like it hadn't been redecorated since 1975!* is an independent clause, you cannot use a comma. This creates what is called a comma splice, so eliminate answer choice G. No coordinating conjunction (*so*) should be used with a semicolon to join independent clauses. Eliminate answer choice F. Using parentheses as in answer choice H complicates the sentence and takes emphasis away from the writer's exclamatory reaction to the décor of the hotel room.

69. **The best answer is C.** The adjective *grim* must modify a noun. Answer choices A, B, and D can be eliminated because they are all verb forms.

70. **The best answer is G.** Rusty and *flimsy* are coordinate adjectives, meaning they modify *antenna* in a similar way. Coordinate adjectives can be separated using *and* or a comma. Answer choices H and J have neither, so eliminate them. However, no comma should come between the modifiers and the noun, so eliminate answer choice F.

71. **The best answer is A.** The verb *reminded* suggests that the television was *kept* in the past. Eliminate answer choices B (future), C (present emphatic), and D (bare or present plural form).

72. **The best answer is J.** It makes the most sense to place Sentence 5 immediately before Sentence 4, because Sentence 5 introduces the *kitchenette* and Sentence 4 provides some additional information about the *kitchenette*. The sentence would be inappropriate placed anywhere else in the paragraph.

73. **The best answer is B.** The writer and her friend are originally very disappointed with the condition of the motel room. However, they decide to *make the best of it and enjoy* themselves. This suggests that they took a bad situation and turned it into a good one. The selection that best acknowledges this shift is answer choice B.

74. **The best answer is J.** This question requires you to identify the main idea of the essay. The essay is primarily about the difficulties that the friends encountered on their trip and how they ended up staying at a subpar motel. Even though the motel was called the Starfish Inn, any information included in the passage about the animal starfish would be irrelevant.

75. **The best answer is C.** Although the essay does provide an example of what could go wrong if you don't make reservations before going on vacation, it does not fully discuss possible hazards of being unprepared for a vacation. The essay is a humorous account of being forced to stay at a dilapidated motel, answer choice C.

Reading Test Explanations

PASSAGE I

1. **The best answer is C.** Granny makes this statement in response to Sheila's comment that, once Martin goes to school, "it will all be so much easier." This suggests that Granny was not convinced that school would challenge Martin effectively. The other answer choices are not supported by the passage.

2. **The best answer is G.** During the conversation Granny says, "I know you're tired from working long hours, but Martin isn't reciting—he's reading!" You can infer that Granny believes Sheila is too overworked to recognize Martin's gift, answer choice G.

3. **The best answer is A.** When Martin's mother says, "He even turns the pages. It's very cute!" she indicates that she doesn't actually think that he can read. This is the best example of the idea that she is unaware of his abilities. The other answer choices do not reflect Sheila's ignorance of her son's reading ability.

4. **The best answer is H.** The context indicates that Sheila and Granny are having a discussion about Granny's care of Martin, and that "it" will get easier when Martin starts school.

5. **The best answer is C.** Throughout the passage, Granny is clearly referred to as Martin's grandmother, so answer choice D should be eliminated. It is also made clear that Granny is Sheila's mother. Therefore, since Sheila is Martin's mother, Granny must be Martin's maternal grandmother, answer choice C.

6. **The best answer is F.** At the end of the passage, Martin's mother agrees that she will start finding out how to get to America with Martin. This best supports answer choice F.

7. **The best answer is D.** Sheila states in the passage, "I'll start finding out what I need to do to get Martin and me to America." This suggests that she understands the importance of going to America and will probably do whatever she can to help Martin succeed. The other answer choices are not supported by the details in the passage.

8. **The best answer is J.** The first paragraph states that Martin's brothers are selfish boys, who "let Martin fend for himself" and "made him the target of their pranks." This suggests that Martin's brothers cared more for themselves than they did

for Martin. The other answer choices are not supported by the passage.

9. **The best answer is C.** The second paragraph shows the trouble that Granny has taking care of Martin because she is old and lacks the energy to keep up with him. This is a conflict in the story because Granny must now decide upon another course of action. The rest of the story tells about Granny's resolution of this conflict.

10. **The best answer is J.** The first paragraph states that "Martin spent most of his childhood in a tropical paradise" but that his "early life was difficult." The word *paradise* most often refers to a delightful or beautiful place. In this case, however, despite the fact that the island of Barbados contains the natural beauty associated with a paradise, the living conditions were not so delightful. This best supports answer choice J.

PASSAGE II

11. **The best answer is D.** The word "engagement" can refer to an "encounter or a battle." The context of the passage supports answer choice D.

12. **The best answer is H.** The word "fanfare" suggests a "display" of some sort. The passage indicates that Lee wanted to take advantage of an opportunity to advance into Northern territory.

13. **The best answer is D.** According to the passage, "Soldiers obeyed Lee's order to refrain from violence and pillaging, so for several days the townspeople maintained tacit compliance and sold food, clothes, and shoes to Southern troops." These details best support answer choice D.

14. **The best answer is G.** The author uses the word "grand" to describe the large loss of life in the Battle of Gettysburg. "Massive" means "large in scale, amount, or degree," so it is the best choice.

15. **The best answer is D.** The passage mentions "devastating artillery bombardment," "battle fatigued soldiers," and "infantry assault" as reasons for the failure of Pickett's Charge.

16. **The best answer is G.** By using the phrase "mile of men," the author implies that there were many soldiers. When the author says that "the mile of men had narrowed nearly to half," he is indicating that the number of soldiers had been significantly reduced during the battle.

17. **The best answer is A.** Allegory suggests symbolism. Because the author is not speaking of literal water, but instead is using the phrase "high water

mark" to refer to the greatest number of Confederate soldiers, he is using the phrase allegorically.

18. The best answer is F. Passage A mentions several battles or engagements but does not describe any specific battle, whereas Passage B focuses primarily on a description of the Battle of Gettysburg.

19. The best answer is C. One of the themes throughout both passages is the large loss of life that resulted from the many battles fought during the Civil War.

20. The best answer is F. Passage A introduces the topic of Civil War battles and the great number of casualties that resulted. Passage B expands upon that notion with a description of one particular battle.

PASSAGE III

21. The best answer is A. The narrator states in the introduction that "the unworldly experience continues to haunt my memory as I recall the unflinching gazes of Pietro Perugino's subjects staring blankly at me as I admired the power and beauty of the great Italian Renaissance master's most famous works of art." Although the narrator briefly speaks about the work of other painters in relation to Perugino, this is not the focus of the paragraph. The narrator is also not impartial about the work of Perugino. In fact, the narrator admits that Perugino is one of his favorite painters. The passage also tells very little about Perugino's life outside of his contributions to art. Eliminate answer choices B, C, and D.

22. The best answer is J. The passage does not mention Donatello as a painter. However, all of the other answer choices are explicitly identified as painters in the passage.

23. The best answer is D. Throughout the passage the narrator discussed his or her strong feelings about Perugino's art. The answer choice that best supports this main idea is answer choice D.

24. The best answer is G. *Ingenuity* is another word for *creativity* or *inventiveness*. The narrator is acknowledging that despite his or her admiration for Perugino's work, it lacked the originality of Botticelli.

25. The best answer is C. The narrator states, "Although the brilliance of all of the Italian Renaissance masters is undeniable, the aweinspiring beauty of Michelangelo's work or the subtle detail of da Vinci's *Mona Lisa* cannot match the simple passion evident in Perugino's paintings." Even though Perugino's work may not show some of the technical skill of other Renaissance painters, the narrator believes Perugino's work outshines the more complicated pieces because of his devotion to and passion for his craft.

26. The best answer is J. The use of the word *eclipsed* suggests that the work of Renoir and Manet was overshadowed by Perugino's work.

27. The best answer is A. All of the following quotes appear in the passage: "In that moment, my admiration for artists like Renoir and Manet of the French Impressionist Movement, was eclipsed by the austere exquisiteness of these fifteenth-century paintings," "cannot match the simple passion evident in Perugino's paintings," and "Perugino also experimented with depth, and he rivaled Leonardo da Vinci in his ability to create a definite background and foreground." These statements best support answer choice A. Abstraction is not mentioned in the passage.

28. The best answer is G. The narrator writes, "I remember feeling slightly disconcerted as I looked up at the unsmiling saints, the Virgin Mary, and even Jesus as I wandered through the hushed halls of the museum." *Disconcerted* is a synonym for *unsettled*.

29. The best answer is B. The passage states that "Perugino also experimented with depth, and he rivaled Leonardo da Vinci in his ability to create a definite background and foreground." This suggests that he was as talented as Leonardo da Vinci at creating depth, which is not a criticism.

30. The best answer is F. The passage states that "The work of da Vinci and Michelangelo is seen on postcards and reprinted on cheap posters everywhere because of its universal appeal." The author does not mention Manet in the discussion about postcard and poster reprints.

PASSAGE IV

31. The best answer is B. The passage begins with the author presenting general information about the porcupine and its behavior; this is followed by a discussion of its habitat and concludes by talking about the ways in which porcupines are useful to humans. Answer choice B contains the broadest survey of the information presented within the passage.

32. **The best answer is J.** The first paragraph states that "the porcupine's mere outward appearance provides more than adequate reason for it rarely to become alarmed or excited." The passage goes on to describe the porcupine as a "threatening creature," which suggests that its appearance is what makes it threatening. The other answer choices are not supported by the passage.

33. **The best answer is C.** According to the passage, the porcupine, "unlike most other animals in the wild," has a threatening appearance that allows it to remain unexcited in the face of danger. The other answer choices are not supported by details in the passage.

34. **The best answer is G.** The author's statement that "the porcupine's mere outward appearance provides more than adequate reason for it rarely to become alarmed or excited" suggests that the porcupine moves slowly because it has no reason to move quickly, answer choice G.

35. **The best answer is B.** Information in the passage indicates that "a noseful or mouthful of porcupine quills" can cause "excruciating pain." This best supports answer choice B.

36. **The best answer is G.** According to the passage, the Yukon Department of Environment considers the porcupine useful, and believes that it has been and can be "appreciated by many." The passage goes on to give examples of the utility of the porcupine quill. This best supports answer choice G.

37. **The best answer is A.** The topic of the second paragraph is the danger of the porcupine's quills—specifically that these quills can become imbedded and cause serious pain. This idea is best summed up in answer choice A.

38. **The best answer is G.** According to the passage, some animals "are able to break down the porcupine's powerful defense system by carefully turning the porcupine over onto its back, exposing its soft and vulnerable underbelly. Bobcats, cougars, and coyotes are especially adept at this technique and pose a major threat to the porcupine."

39. **The best answer is B.** According to the passage, if a dog gets a noseful or mouthful of quills, it should be "tended to right away," so eliminate answer choice C. The passage goes on to say that extraction of the quills can "relieve the excruciating pain," so it makes sense that imbedded porcupine quills can be very painful, answer choice B.

40. **The best answer is J.** The scientific name for the porcupine is *Erethizon dorsatum*, which is Latin for "irritable back." The other answer choices are mentioned in the passage, but not in reference to the scientific name of the porcupine.

PART III

SAT Strategies and Concept Review

The SAT Reading Test

What is the SAT Reading test?

The SAT includes a 65-minute Reading test designed to assess your

proficiency in reading and comprehending a broad range of high-quality, appropriately challenging literary and informational texts in the content areas of U.S. and world literature, history/social studies, and science.

The SAT Reading test consists of four passages, each 500–750 words long. You are to read the passages and answer multiple-choice questions about

- the purpose and main idea of the passage
- the meaning and purpose of particular words and phrases in context
- the inferences that can be justifiably drawn from the passage
- the tone and attitude conveyed by the author

Additionally, some passages with a common theme are paired and accompanied by questions about

- points of agreement or disagreement between the paired passages
- differences in tone or emphasis between the paired passages

Also, some of the passages will be accompanied by tables or graphs and questions about

- how to interpret the data represented in the table or graph
- how to incorporate these data appropriately into the passage

How is it used?

Colleges use your SAT Reading test score as a measure of your ability to perform demanding college-level reading tasks. The SAT Reading test score represents one-half of your Evidence-Based Reading and Writing score. The other half of this score comes from the Writing and Language test.

Sound intimidating? It's not.

There are only four rules of analytical reading to learn in order to ace the SAT Reading test, and the lessons in this chapter will give you the knowledge and practice you need to master them.

The Core Analytical Reading Skills

Lesson 1: Learn to read analytically

Which is correct?

A.   *The SAT Reading test is primarily a test of your multiple-choice test-taking skill.*
B.   *The SAT Reading test is primarily a test of your analytical reading skill.*
C.   *The SAT Reading test is primarily a test of your literary reading skill.*

Although basic test-taking skills are helpful, they won't get you very far. Acing the SAT Reading test requires solid **analytical reading skills**, that is, the ability to **extract the key information** from any passage and **to identify its evidence**. Specifically, you should be able to read any SAT passage on any topic and determine its

* purpose
* central idea
* structure
* functional elements
* tone

It's important to remember that the SAT Reading test is *not* **a literary skills test**. You may spend a lot of time in English class learning to

* explore connections between a text and its cultural context

* evaluate the emotional effect of a literary piece
* explore abstract ideas that are implicit in a work, such as "the concept of utopia"
* find examples of symbolism, foreshadowing, and other subtle and figurative literary elements

But these literary skills, while important for your enjoyment and edification, are not tested by the SAT Reading test.

Although it is helpful to know a few important **test-taking skills**, just knowing these tricks won't get you very far. The SAT Reading test is essentially a test of **analytical reading skill**, *not* literary **reading skills**.

According to the College Board, the SAT Reading test is **evidence-based**. That is, it specifically assesses your ability to justify your responses with **literal evidence** from the passage and **quantitative evidence** from associated tables or graphs. Therefore, be ready to supply the **evidence** for any answers you give.

Lesson 2: Get your mind right

Which is correct?

   A. *The SAT Reading passages are chosen to be as difficult and boring as possible.*

   B. *The SAT Reading passages are chosen because they represent the kinds of prose students are most likely to encounter in a college liberal arts curriculum.*

The answer, despite popular belief, is B. The SAT Reading passages are not chosen by sadists. They are selected to represent the kind of reading you will do in college. Don't begin the SAT Reading Test with the attitude, "Oh no, not another tedious and pointless SAT reading passage!" This will only sabotage your performance by creating a negative self-fulfilling prophecy.

How well you do on the SAT Reading test depends very much on the mindset you bring to the test.

If you expect a passage to be tedious and pointless, it will be, because you will miss its interesting key points. If instead you expect to learn something new and interesting, you will remain more focused and engaged and attack the questions much more confidently and accurately.

Keep an open mind and—we promise—you'll learn something new from every SAT you take.

How do you avoid "spacing out?"

Many students occasionally "space out" on high-pressure reading tests like the SAT: their eyes scan over the words, but the words don't go in the brain. The best way to avoid space-outs is to **master the skills of active reading**. When your brain is active and engaged, it can't "space out." The heart of active reading is focusing on the **analytical questions** that we will discuss in the upcoming lessons.

The Three Key Questions

Lesson 3: Ask, "What is the purpose of this passage?"

To comprehend a passage analytically, you must first categorize it in terms of which three categories?

    A. *Fiction, nonfiction, or poetry*
    B. *Exposition, rhetoric, or narrative*
    C. *History, science, or humanities*

The correct answer is B. Don't worry so much about whether the passage is fiction or nonfiction, or if the topic is unfamiliar to you. You need a plan of attack for any passage the SAT throws your way. Strong analytical reading begins with asking, **"What is the overall purpose of this passage?"** Any well-written piece of prose has one of three possible purposes corresponding to the following categories:

- **Expository prose** presents **objective information** and is organized around a **guiding question**, such as "What happened in the Battle of Bull Run?" or "What is polarized light, and what is it used for?" Examples of expository prose include news articles and science textbooks.
- **Rhetorical prose** presents **an author's personal point of view** and is organized around a **thesis**, such as "We have an exaggerated perception of gang violence," or "Hiking is good for the soul." Examples of rhetorical prose include Op-Ed essays, blog posts, and some magazine articles.
- **Narrative prose** presents **a fictional or nonfictional story** and is organized around a **protagonist and a transformative struggle**, such as "Jean Valjean struggles to redeem himself," or "King Lear struggles to establish a legacy." Examples of narrative prose include memoirs, short stories, biographies, and novels.

As you read any SAT Reading passage, first ask, **"What is its overall purpose: to present objective information** (expository), **to present a point of view** (rhetorical), **or to tell a story** (narrative)?"

You can often determine overall purpose from the introduction or the first paragraph. For instance, if a passage is described as a *discussion* or *description,* it's likely to be expository. If it is described as a *speech* or an *essay,* it's probably rhetorical. If it is described as an excerpt from a *memoir* or *novel,* then it's probably narrative.

But **be careful.** Authors often combine different modes of prose. For instance, an essay arguing for tougher gun laws (rhetorical purpose) might tell a heart-wrenching story (narrative element) to make the point. Similarly, a short story (narrative purpose) might include a lengthy description (expository element) of the town in which it is set.

Always confirm your theory about purpose by carefully reading the final paragraph. If the final paragraph focuses on describing an interesting fact, the passage is probably expository. If it focuses on a proposal, evaluation, or suggestion, the passage is probably rhetorical. If it describes a person's resolution of a problem, the passage is probably a narrative. **Most passages confirm their overall purpose in the final paragraph.**

Lesson 4: Ask, "What is the central idea of this passage?"

What is the best way to determine the central idea of a passage?

   A. *Read the first paragraph, which always summarizes the main idea.*
   B. *Read the topic sentence of the final paragraph.*
   C. *It depends on the passage type and structure.*

The correct answer is C. Although the first and last paragraphs often contain key information, sometimes the first paragraph or two simply provide background information or summarize a misconception to be refuted. Sometimes a passage doesn't get around to the central idea until the third or fourth paragraph.

> **Once you have determined the general purpose of the passage, focus immediately on finding the central idea.** The purpose and central idea are intimately linked.
>
> • The central idea of any **expository essay** is a **guiding question**, such as "What is the carbon cycle?"
> • The central idea of any **rhetorical essay** is a **thesis**, such as "Perseverance is more important to success than skill is."
> • The central idea of any **narrative** is the **protagonist's transformative struggle**, such as "The narrator discovers how to be an artist."
>
> **The central idea is often, but not always, revealed at the beginning of the passage and reinforced at the end of the passage.** Sometimes your first guess about the main idea, based on the first paragraph, may be wrong and need to be revised.

Consider this excerpt and the question that follows:

Without some appreciation of common large numbers, it's impossible to react with the proper skepticism to terrifying reports that more than a million American kids are kidnapped each year, or with the proper sobriety to a warhead carrying a megaton of explosive power—the equivalent of a million tons (or two billion pounds) of TNT.

And if you don't have some feeling for probabilities, automobile accidents might seem a relatively minor problem of local travel, whereas being killed by terrorists might seem to be a major risk when going overseas. As often observed, however, the 45,000 people killed annually on American roads are approximately equal in number to all American dead in the Vietnam War. On the other hand,

the seventeen Americans killed by terrorists in 1985 were among the 28 million of us who traveled abroad that year—that's one chance in 1.6 million of becoming a victim . . .

The primary purpose of this passage is to

   A) warn against the dangers associated with daily living in the United States
   B) compare the costs of war-related activities to the costs of domestic activities
   C) discuss common misunderstandings about statistical data
   D) propose solutions to some problems in American domestic and foreign policy

Most students get this question wrong, because they focus too much on **specific details** and not enough on **overall purpose** and **logical structure**.

So what is the central idea in this passage? If you look at some of the passage details, such as the references to car accidents and kidnapping, you might be reminded of *the dangers associated with daily living* or the *cost of domestic activities* or even *domestic policy problems*. If you notice the references to warheads, the Vietnam War, and terrorism, you might be reminded of *war-related activities* or *American foreign policy problems*. For these reasons, choices A, B, and D might all seem like good answers.

But they are all wrong.

Consider choice A. Is kidnapping mentioned in order to *warn against danger*? No: the author says that the *proper* response to the *terrifying reports that more than a million American kids are kidnapped each year* is not fear and caution, but *skepticism*. In fact, his point is that if we had *some appreciation of common large numbers*, we would see that this statistic is preposterous.

How about choice B? The statement that *the 45,000 people killed annually on American roads are approximately equal in number to all American dead in the Vietnam War* seems to be comparing *the costs of war-related activities to the costs of domestic activities*. But is this the *primary purpose of the passage*? No, this statistic is mentioned only to make a broader point: that it is irrational to fear terrorism more than daily driving, and that this irrationality is due, in least in part, to our lack of *feeling about probabilities*.

Now look at choice D. Does the passage *propose any solutions* to the problems of kidnapping, terrorism, nuclear weapons, car accidents, or war? Certainly not in these first two paragraphs. More important, these paragraphs suggest a very different overall purpose.

The point of these first two paragraphs is that *[w]ithout some appreciation of common large numbers* and a *feeling for probabilities*, we will overreact to some dangers and underreact to others. In other words, there is some danger inherent in our *common misunderstandings about statistical data*. Therefore, the best answer is choice C.

How to attack purpose questions

Many SAT Reading questions ask about the **purpose** of particular words, phrases, or references. Here are some examples:

> The author uses the word "debacle" (line 3) in order to emphasize her belief that . . .

> The quotation in lines 42–51 primarily serves to . . .

To attack these questions, first remind yourself of the **overall purpose and central idea** of the passage, and remember that **every portion of the passage must help convey the central idea of the passage.**

Consider this question about the "innumeracy" passage that is the source of the earlier quote:

> The author mentions the work of Drs. Kronlund and Phillips (lines 53–58) primarily in order to
>
> A) warn against the risks of certain medical procedures
>
> B) highlight a promising medical breakthrough
>
> C) demonstrate the fallibility of medical experts
>
> D) dispute a common medical theory

Even without reading lines 53–58, you can see which choices don't fit with the overall purpose and central idea that we identified in the previous question. Since the primary purpose of this passage is to "discuss common misunderstandings about statistical data," the reference to *the work of Drs. Kronlund and Phillips* must serve this primary purpose in some way. Choices B and D are not strongly connected to the understanding of statistical data. Choices A and C, however, are plausible answers because *warning against risks* often involves understanding the data that show the likelihood of those risks, and *the fallibility of medical experts* might include their inability to understand and interpret statistics (which is precisely the main theme of the essay).

Lesson 5: Ask, "What is the structure of this passage?"

Here is a sample SAT Reading passage, with some notes about its **functional structure**.

This passage is adapted from Cleveland Hickman,
Larry Roberts, and Allan Larson, Integrated Principles
of Zoology. ©2001 The McGraw-Hill Companies.

Line

    In ancient times, people commonly
believed that new life could arise not only by
parental reproduction, but also, on occasion, by
spontaneous generation from nonliving material.

5 For example, frogs appeared to arise from damp
earth, mice from putrefied matter, insects from
dew, and maggots from decaying meat. Warmth,
moisture, sunlight, and even starlight often
were mentioned as factors that encouraged

10 spontaneous generation of living organisms.

> **Misconception** about the origin of life: spontaneous generation.

    One of the early efforts to synthesize
organisms in the laboratory can be seen in a
recipe for making mice given by the Belgian plant
nutritionist Jean Baptiste van Helmont (1648):

15   . . . press a piece of underwear soiled with
sweat together with some wheat in an open jar,
after about 21 days the odor changes and the
ferment. . . . changes the wheat into mice . . . not
small mice, not even miniature adults or aborted

20 mice, but adult mice emerge!

> **Example** of this misconception: recipe for synthesizing adult mice from soiled underwear.

    In 1861, Louis Pasteur demonstrated that,
in fact, living organisms cannot so easily arise
spontaneously from nonliving matter. In his
experiments, Pasteur introduced fermentable

25 material into a flask with a long S-shaped neck
that was open to the air. The flask and its contents
were boiled to kill any microorganisms, then
cooled and left undisturbed. No fermentation
could occur because new microorganisms

30 could not enter through the neck. But when
the neck was removed, microorganisms in the
air could enter the fermentable material and
proliferate. Thus, Pasteur showed that life came
from previously existing organisms and their

35 reproductive elements, such as eggs and spores or,
in the case of van Helmont's "recipe," adult mice
that crept into the jar. Announcing his results to
the French Academy, Pasteur proclaimed, "Never
will the doctrine of spontaneous generation arise

40 from this mortal blow."

> **Refutation** of theory of spontaneous generation by a clever experiment.

But Pasteur, for all his brilliance, wasn't entirely correct. The first "life," if we can call it that, appears to have assembled over the course of millions of years of random collisions of
45 nonliving molecules in the chemical-rich cauldron of early Earth, until, by chance, very basic self-replicating units formed. These first self-replicating units, which arose almost 4 billion years ago, are most likely the ancestors we share
50 with every living thing on earth today. But with no scientist to witness it, how can we know that the dawn of life happened that way? The evidence is embedded in the complex molecules common to all living things—DNA, RNA, proteins, lipids,
55 hormones—which can be painstakingly traced back to simpler chemicals that most likely preceded them in the family tree. Even more profoundly, astrophysicists can now trace the building blocks of life—carbon, nitrogen, and
60 oxygen—to a spectacular birth inside ancient exploding stars!

Implication of rare biogenesis over millions of years: it seems to have happened only once, so all life is related.

To read analytically, you must pay attention to the functional structure of the passage. In other words, think about how **each paragraph** serves the central idea.

Notice that, in the passage above, the notes indicate that the first paragraph *describes a misconception*, the second *provides an example of that misconception*, the third *provides a refutation of that misconception*, and the fourth *describes an implication of the corrected theory*. All of these paragraphs serve the central purpose of *describing the history and implications of a biological theory*.

The **structure** of a passage depends very much on its **purpose**.

Expository essays can be structured in many possible ways in order to answer the guiding question.

They may include background information, illustrations of concepts, examples of general claims, relevant data, anecdotes, or discussions of implications. Of course, any of these elements may be omitted, supplemented, or rearranged.

Narratives have a fairly consistent structure: (1) the struggle is introduced, (2) the struggle is developed, and (3) the struggle is resolved, transforming the protagonist. The details may differ dramatically from narrative to narrative, but the overall structure probably will not.

Rhetorical essays can also be structured in many possible ways. A **rhetorical argument** is likely to describe a position, then refute it with a counterargument. A **rhetorical narrative** tells a story in order to highlight a particular point of view. Rhetorical essay can include paragraphs dedicated to logical analysis of a claim, explanation, illustration, discussion of implications, modification of a claim, and so on.

The SAT Writing and Language Test

What is the SAT Writing and Language test?

The SAT includes a 35-minute Writing and Language test designed to assess your

> *proficiency in revising and editing a range of texts in a variety of content areas, both academic and career related, for expression of ideas and for conformity to the conventions of Standard Written English grammar, usage and punctuation.*

The Writing and Language test consists of four passages, each 400–450 words long, in the categories of careers, social studies, humanities, and science. You are to analyze underlined portions of each passage and to determine whether they need to be revised according to the standards of

- parallel structure
- verb, modifier, and pronoun agreement
- standard idiom
- logical comparisons
- word choice
- verb tense, mood, and voice
- logical transitions
- coordination of ideas
- punctuation

You are also asked more general editorial questions, such as

- whether a certain sentence adds to or detracts from the cohesiveness of a paragraph
- where a new sentence should be placed for maximum effectiveness
- whether a particular passage or paragraph has the effect the author intends

How is it used?

Colleges use your SAT Writing and Language test score as a measure of your ability to write clearly and effectively. Good writing skills are essential to success in the liberal arts and sciences. The Writing and Language test score represents one-half of your Evidence-Based Reading and Writing Score. The other half of this score comes from the Reading test.

Sound intimidating? It's not.

There are several rules to learn in order to ace the SAT Writing and Language test, and the lessons in this chapter will give you the knowledge you need to master them.

Rule 1: Don't Sweat the Small Stuff

Lesson 1: Know the seven things to *NOT* worry about

1. Don't worry about split infinitives

Which is correct?

   A.   *Here are seven things to **not** worry about.*
   B.   *Here are seven things **not** to worry about.*

Sentence A includes a **split infinitive**: the infinitive *to worry* has an adverb (*not*) wedged inside it. Although the SAT probably won't test your skill for "unsplitting" infinitives, you should still do it as a matter of politeness to the grammar scolds, for whom they are the verbal equivalent of chewing aluminum foil. You can usually just shift the adverb over a little bit, as in sentence B, and make everyone happy.

But sometimes it's not so easy to unsplit infinitives without destroying the tone or meaning of the sentence. For instance, try unsplitting the infinitive in *The company plans to more than double its revenue next year.* Or, better yet, just don't worry about it, since it won't be on the SAT.

2. Don't worry (too much) about *who* vs. *whom*

Which is correct?

   A.   *To **who** should I give your condolences?*
   B.   *To **whom** should I give your condolences?*

The *who*/*whom* distinction is the same as the *he*/*him* and *they*/*them* distinction: the first pronoun in each pair has the **subjective case** (Lesson 21), and so is used as the *subject* of a verb, and the second has the **objective case**, and so is used as the *object* of a verb or preposition. Since the pronoun in the sentence above is the object of the preposition *to*, sentence B is correct.

Notice, however, that the pronoun *you* can be used as either a subject *or* an object. It represents a "merger" between the subjective *thou* and the objective *thee* from Elizabethan English. (Remember Shakespeare?) Likewise, *whom* seems to be in the process of merging with *who*. For instance, even Standard English allows a sentence like *Who are you talking to?* rather than insisting on the rather uptight-sounding *To whom are you talking?*

The bottom line? Chances are, your SAT won't ask you to choose between *who* and *whom*. But if it does, just remember that the *who*/*whom* distinction is the same as the *they*/*them* and *he*/*him* distinctions. And if you're still stuck, just go with *who*.

3. Don't worry about *that* vs. *which*

Which is correct?

   A.   *Second Federal is the only bank in town **which** does not finance commercial mortgages.*

   B.   *Second Federal is the only bank in town **that** does not finance commercial mortgages.*

Technically, sentence B is correct because the phrase *that does not finance commercial mortgages* is a "restrictive clause," that is, it modifies the noun *bank* by attaching a defining characteristic to it. If a modifying clause is "restrictive" (that is, it conveys defining information about the noun), it should use *that*. Alternately, if the clause is "nonrestrictive" (that is, it conveys incidental or nondefining information about the noun), it should use *which*. Helpful tip: nonrestrictive modifying clauses are almost always preceded by a comma, as in *The speech, which lasted only three minutes, secured her reputation as a master orator.*

Bottom line: the SAT will probably not expect you to distinguish restrictive from nonrestrictive clauses, so don't stress out about *that* versus *which* on the SAT.

4. Don't worry about starting sentences with *Because*, *And*, or *But*

Which is correct?

   A.   *Because we don't know when Jennie will arrive, we can't make dinner reservations yet.*
   B.   *We can't make dinner reservations yet because we don't know when Jennie will arrive.*

Ms. Bumthistle (everyone's fifth grade English teacher) probably told you that it's a cardinal sin to start a sentence with *Because*, *And*, or *But*. But it's not nice to lie to children. In fact, either sentence above is fine. The SAT frequently includes perfectly good sentences that start with *Because*. But if you want to avoid annoying the Ms. Bumthistles of the world, avoid the practice in your own writing if it's not too much trouble.

5. Don't worry about disappearing *that*s

Which is correct?

   A.   *I really love the sweater you gave me.*
   B.   *I really love the sweater **that** you gave me.*

Both of the sentences above are acceptable in Standard Written English. So, if *that* isn't necessary, why would we ever include it? Because it takes some of the burden away from *sweater*, which is an object in the first clause (*I really love the sweater*) as well as an object of the second clause (*You gave me [the sweater]*). By including *that*, we separate the two ideas more clearly. But since very few people are confused by the dual role of *sweater* in the first sentence, *that* is not strictly necessary.

Bottom line: don't worry about a missing *that*, as long as the resulting sentence still makes sense.

6. Don't worry about "parallel ellipsis"

Which is correct?

A. *The Republicans reacted to the speech with sustained applause; the Democrats, however, reacted to it with studied silence.*

B. *The Republicans reacted to the speech with sustained applause; the Democrats, studied silence.*

Both of the sentences above are grammatically correct. Sentence B, however, is more concise because it takes advantage of "parallel ellipsis." Ellipsis simply means the omission of words that are implied by context. In this case, the parallel structure of the two clauses allows the reader to "fill in" the missing words.

When you read a sentence like B, you might think that the missing words are a grammatical mistake. But if the context clearly implies the missing words, you can leave them out.

You might notice that, in sentence B, the comma plays an unusual role. Usually, commas are used to separate items in a list, to separate modifying phrases from clauses, or (with conjunctions) to separate clauses. Here, however, the comma is analogous to the apostrophe in *can't*: just as the apostrophe holds the place of the missing letters from *cannot*, so the comma in sentence B holds the place of the missing words (*however, reacted to it with*) from sentence A. Without that comma to suggest the ellipsis, the sentence would sound very strange indeed.

7. Don't worry (too much) about *good* versus *well* or *bad* versus *badly*

Which is correct?

A. *Peter performed good.*

B. *Peter performed well.*

Here, *performed* is an action verb. Any word that modifies the manner of an action verb is an *adverb*. Since *good* cannot function as an adverb in Standard English, only choice B is correct.

Which is correct?

C. *I don't feel good.*

D. *I don't feel well.*

Here, *feel* is a linking verb rather than an action verb: that is, it links the subject to an essential adjective, as in *The sky is blue.* So does this mean that C is right and D is wrong? No—they are both grammatically and semantically correct, since *well* can also act as an adjective, meaning "in good health." The two sentences are essentially equivalent to *I am not [feeling] good* and *I am not well.*

Which is correct?

E. *I feel bad for you.*

F. *I feel badly for you.*

Here, despite what your know-it-all friends might say, E is correct and F is wrong, since *badly* can only function as an adverb. Saying *I feel bad for you* is like saying *I feel sorry for you.* You wouldn't say *I feel sorrily for you*, would you?

It's important to know the difference between adjectives and adverbs (Lesson 14), and between action verbs and linking verbs.

But the SAT is probably not going to ask you about *good* versus *well* or *bad* versus *badly*.

Rule 2: Strengthen the Core

Lesson 2: Identify your clauses, modifiers, and conjunctions

To analyze a sentence grammatically, first identify the **core** of each **clause**. A clause is any phrase that includes a subject and verb, such as *The chair* [subject] *broke* [verb]. A clause can also contain modifiers and modifying phrases that, while informative, do not define the central idea of the clause. When we "trim" these modifiers from the clause, what remains is the **core**. Every strong sentence is built around a strong core.

The **core** of every clause conveys its central idea. For instance, consider the sentence

As the sun slowly set, the canvas of the sails glowed like freshly bruised skin.

If we trim away the modifiers, we still retain the core idea:

The canvas glowed.

Consider these two sentences:

A. *Go!*
B. *Although generally regarded as the most daunting course in the undergraduate science curriculum, Introduction to Organic Chemistry not only provides a necessary foundation in the principles of physical chemistry, but also introduces students to important experimental methods at the heart of today's most promising areas of medical research.*

Sentence A is the shortest in the English language. It has everything necessary to convey a complete thought: a verb (*go*) and its subject (the implied subject *you*). Since it is in the **imperative mood** (Lesson 30), the subject is assumed to be the person being addressed and does not need to be stated.

So here's how we can analyze sentence A:

You [subject] *go* [verb]*!*

Main clauses can also be elaborated with modifiers, or linked to other clauses with conjunctions.

Sentence B is a bit more complicated. The main clause includes a compound predicate, so it combines two statements with the same subject into one sentence:

Introduction to Organic Chemistry . . . provides a necessary foundation in the principles of physical chemistry . . .

Introduction to Organic Chemistry . . . introduces students to important experimental methods at the heart today's most promising areas of medical research.

So here's how we can analyze sentence B:

Although [subordinating conjunction] *generally regarded as the most daunting course in the undergraduate science curriculum* [participial phrase], *Introduction to Organic Chemistry* [subject] *not only* [conjunction part 1] *provides a necessary foundation in the principles of physical chemistry* [predicate 1], *but also* [conjunction part 2] *introduces students to important experimental methods at the heart of today's most promising areas of medical research* [predicate 2].

If this analysis seems confusing now, don't worry. We'll explain all of these terms in the lessons to come. For now, focus on identifying the **core** of every **clause**. Distinguishing clauses from the rest of the sentence is the first step to becoming a stronger reader and writer.

Lesson 3: Trim every sentence to analyze its core

Consider this sentence:

My chief concern with this budget, which has otherwise been well considered, are the drastic cuts in school funds.

How does it sound? It may sound a little bit off, but why, and how do we improve it? This is where **trimming** comes in.

> Diagnosing and improving sentences requires mastering the skill of **trimming**: reducing the sentence to its **core**, or its essential elements, then analyzing that core.
>
> This is based on a very important rule of grammar: **every sentence must "work" even when its prepositional phrases, interrupters, and other modifiers are eliminated.** That is, it still must convey a grammatically complete idea.

Step 1: Cross out all nonessential prepositional phrases.

A **preposition** is any word that can be used to complete any sentence like these:

The squirrel ran _____ the tree. (e.g. *up, to, around, from, in, by, on, into,* etc.)

I went to the party _____ a brain surgeon. (e.g., *as, with, for,* etc.)

Democracy is government _____ the people. (e.g., *for, of, by,* etc.)

A **prepositional phrase** is the preposition plus the noun phrase that follows it, such as *from sea to shining sea, in the beginning,* and *for the money.*

Our sentence has two nonessential prepositional phrases that we can eliminate:

My chief concern ~~with this budget~~, which has otherwise been well considered, are the drastic cuts ~~in school funds~~.

Step 2: Cross out all interrupting modifiers.

Interrupting modifiers are generally easy to spot because they come between commas or dashes. The sentence should always hold together even when the interrupting modifiers are removed:

My chief concern ~~with this budget, which has otherwise been well considered~~, are the drastic cuts ~~in school funds~~.

Step 3: Cross out any other nonessential modifiers.

Once you learn to identify **participial phrases** (Lesson 12), **appositives** (Lesson 13), and more mundane modifiers like **adjectives** and **adverbs** (Lesson 14), you can trim them from all of your sentences, as well, with one exception: **predicate adjectives**, such as *tired* in the sentence *Karen was tired*, without which the sentence doesn't convey an idea. In our sentence, *chief* and *drastic* can go:

My ~~chief~~ concern ~~with this budget, which has otherwise been well considered~~, are the ~~drastic~~ cuts ~~in school funds~~.

So now we have the core:

My concern are the cuts.

Obviously, the subject and verb **disagree** (Lesson 4): *concern* is a singular subject, but *are* is a plural verb. So you may just want to change the verb: *My concern is the cuts.* But that's no good either, because now the sentence has a **number shift** (Lesson 11): the singular *concern* is equated with the plural *cuts*.

These problems point to an even deeper problem: the most essential part of the sentence, the verb, is very weak. Forms of the verb *to be*, like *is, are, was,* and *were,* are among the weakest verbs in English.

> To improve your writing, first focus on **strengthening and clarifying your verbs**.

This sentence is clearly indicating disapproval, so a more personal subject like *I* and a strong verb of disapproval like *object* would strengthen the sentence:

Although the budget is otherwise well considered, I object to its drastic cuts in school funds.

Notice that this revision not only corrects the grammatical problems, but it also makes the sentence stronger, clearer, and more concise.

Rule 3: Organize the Ideas in Your Paragraphs

Lesson 4: Present your ideas cohesively and with a consistent tone

What's wrong with this paragraph?

The politics of hydraulic fracturing, or "fracking," have obscured both the dangers and the benefits of this new technology. Opponents suggest that the high-pressure fluid used to fracture deep rock formations may contain carcinogens that may seep into groundwater, and that fracking induces earthquakes. Supporters point out that this activity is taking place well below even the deepest aquifers and is well sealed off from human water supplies. The technical term for earthquakes is seismic activity, and the fractures are pretty small, really: only about 1 millimeter or less.

The paragraph starts off well, with a clear topic sentence about the politics of fracking. It then gives a quick summary of the two positions on the topic. With the last sentence, however, the paragraph begins to lose its focus and tone: the phrase *pretty small, really* is too conversational for the tone of this paragraph, and the ideas in the last sentence are not tied logically to the ongoing discussion. Here's a revision that more effectively links to the previous sentence:

They also point out that the seismic activity induced by fracking is minimal: the vast majority of the fractures it induces are less than 1 millimeter wide.

Every **effective** prose paragraph should

- be focused on a topic sentence that develops the central idea of the passage
- explain or illustrate any significant claims
- avoid irrelevant commentary
- maintain a consistent and appropriate tone

On the SAT Writing and Language Test, pay attention to the **cohesiveness** of each paragraph and of the essay as a whole. That is, the essay should have a **consistent tone**, the paragraphs should link together to form a **logical train of thought**, and each paragraph should **develop a single independent idea**.

Some Writing and Language Test questions ask you to consider whether a given sentence should be inserted or deleted, or to find the best location for a given sentence or paragraph. When answering such questions, be sure to **consider the overall tone and logical flow of the passage**, and make sure to **avoid redundancy, irrelevant information, illogical sequencing, and inappropriate shifts in tone**.

Lesson 5: Coordinate your clauses effectively and avoid commas splices

Which is better?

A. *Despite being a best-selling author, Brian Greene is a professor of physics, he is also cofounder of the World Science Festival, and this event draws nearly half a million people each year.*

B. *Cofounded by best-selling author and professor of physics Brian Greene, the World Science Festival draws nearly half a million people each year.*

It's not too hard to see that sentence B seems clearer and more logical than sentence A, but why? The answer is **coordination**. Both sentences contain the same four ideas, but sentence B coordinates those ideas more effectively. Sentence A contains three independent clauses:

. . . Brian Greene is a professor of physics . . .

. . . [Brian Greene] is also cofounder of the World Science Festival . . .

. . . [the World Science Festival] draws nearly half a million people each year . . .

So the reader is left confused: what is the central idea of this sentence? Brian Greene's professorship? His festival? The popularity of the festival? Even worse, the **preposition** *Despite* doesn't make sense, since being a best-selling author doesn't interfere in any obvious way with being a physics professor.

Sentence B, in contrast, packages these ideas to make them easier to digest. The first two ideas are **subordinated** in a **participial phrase**, and the third idea is emphasized as the **independent clause**.

In a **well-coordinated** sentence,

- the central idea is expressed in the main **independent clause**
- secondary ideas are expressed in **subordinate clauses** or **modifying phrases**
- ideas are linked with logically appropriate **conjunctions**, **prepositions**, and **adverbs**

Notice also that the second comma in sentence A is a **comma splice**, joining two independent clauses. That's a no-no.

Avoid **comma splices**. A comma splice is the error of joining two **independent clauses** with only a comma:

Comma splice (wrong):   *We were having a great time, T.J. played his guitar.*

Independent clauses can be joined in one sentence in one of three acceptable ways:

Comma-conjunction: *We were having a great time, but T.J. played his guitar.*
Semicolon: *We were having a great time; T.J. played his guitar.*
Colon: *We were having a great time: T.J. played his guitar.*

These three options coordinate the two clauses in very different ways. The first sentence indicates that T.J.'s guitar *didn't help* the mood; the second indicates that T.J.'s guitar *didn't hurt* the mood; the third indicates that T.J.'s guitar *explained* the mood.

Make sure you know the rules for using **semicolons** and **colons**.

- **Semicolons** should be used only when joining two **independent clauses** (that is, phrases that could stand alone as sentences) that have a **supporting relationship**. For instance: *I can't wait to see you; it feels like I haven't seen you in ages!* (There is an obscure exception to this rule: sometimes semicolons can be used to separate items in a list, if those items include commas. But you will probably never see this usage on the SAT.)
- **Colons** can be used to join independent clauses, but only when the second clause **explains or illustrates** the first clause. For instance: *Our teacher was angry: we were woefully unprepared for the discussion.*
- **Colons** can also be used to introduce an item or list of items that exemplify a noun or pronoun in the preceding clause. For instance: *We were met with several annoyances: the rain, the cold, and the rowdy fans. The miserable conditions left us only one good option: to leave.*
- On the SAT, colons and semicolons **must always be preceded by an independent clause**.

Lesson 6: Give your reader helpful transitions, especially between paragraphs

Consider this transition between paragraphs:

> *. . . and so we should be respectful of other people, even those with whom we disagree, while always striving to eliminate inequities and abuses of power.*
>
> To Kill a Mockingbird *was written by Harper Lee and published in 1960. It portrays the fictional town of Maycomb, Alabama . . .*

The end of the first paragraph makes a bold claim: that we should strive *to eliminate inequities and abuses of power.* But the next paragraph abruptly shifts to mundane facts about the publication of a particular book. Although readers who are familiar with *To Kill a Mockingbird* might have an idea why this author is mentioning it, the author does not provide any helpful transitions to guide the reader into the new paragraph and indicate how the new paragraph connects with previous one. Consider this revision:

> *. . . and so we should be respectful of other people, even those with whom we disagree, while always striving to eliminate inequities and abuses of power.*
>
> *In* To Kill a Mockingbird *(1960), Harper Lee depicts a fictional town, Maycomb, Alabama, that is tainted by such inequities and abuses . . .*

Now we understand the reference better because the author has provided a **helpful paragraph transition**. The phrase *such inequities and abuses* demonstrates clearly that the events in *To Kill a Mockingbird* will illustrate the importance of fighting inequities and abuse, and therefore exemplify the thesis from the previous paragraph.

Provide your readers with helpful paragraph transitions to clarify the links between topic ideas. Keep in mind the common **transitional words and phrases** below.

To extend an idea

indeed	*furthermore*	*moreover*	*in fact*
further	*also*	*beyond that*	*additionally*

To illustrate or specify an idea

for example	*for instance*	*in particular*	*namely*
such as	*especially*	*to illustrate*	*specifically*

To make a comparison or contrast

similarly	*likewise*	*actually*	*nevertheless*
however	*although*	*despite*	*on the other hand*

To show consequence

as a result	*so*	*thus*	*subsequently*
therefore	*hence*	*accordingly*	*for this reason*

To provide explanation or reason

this is because	*since*	*thus*	*the reason is that*
how	*because*	*why*	*as*

Lesson 7: Make your cross-references clear

Consider these sentences from our "fracking" essay:

. . . The opponents of fracking are correct to ask questions about the safety and sustainability of this process. Could it poison the local water supply with carcinogens? Can we spare the vast amount of injection water it requires? Can we safely recycle its wastewater? Could it be introducing more methane into the water supply than would naturally be present? Could it be causing potentially dangerous seismic activity? But this also must be followed by careful, scientific, and impartial investigation, not mere fear-mongering.

Each of the five questioning sentences contains the pronoun *it*, which makes a "cross-reference" to a noun in the first sentence, namely, *fracking* (or, equivalently, *process*). The last sentence also includes a cross-referencing pronoun, *this*. But to what does it refer? It doesn't seem to be referring to fracking anymore; that wouldn't make sense. Nor does it make sense to refer to the other singular nouns in previous sentences, like *methane, water supply,* or *seismic activity*. So the reader may be left a bit confused. Here, we need to revise to clarify the cross-reference:

*But **this questioning** must be followed by careful, scientific, and impartial investigation, not mere fear-mongering.*

When referring to concepts introduced in previous sentences, using **pronouns** will often help you be concise, but **make sure your cross-references are clear**. Sometimes clarity may require you to replace the "cross-referencing" pronouns with more precise nouns.

On the SAT Writing and Language Test, if an underlined sentence or phrase includes a pronoun or other "reference word," always ask, "Is the reference clear and precise?" If not, choose an option that clarifies it.

Rule 4: Use Parallel Structure

Lesson 8: Understand the Law of Parallelism

Which is better?

  A. *In the '70s and '80s, high school math teachers taught almost exclusively by lecture; today, more cooperative and project-based methods are likely to be employed.*

  B. *In the '70s and '80s, high school math teachers taught almost exclusively by lecture; today, they are more likely to use cooperative and project-based methods.*

Which is better?

  C. *Ms. Kelly always tried to provide clear instructions that showed respect and were fair to all of her students.*

  D. *Ms. Kelly always tried to provide instructions that were clear, respectful, and fair to all of her students.*

Sentences A and C don't seem glaringly wrong, but B and D sound a bit better. Why? **Parallelism.**

The Law of Parallelism

When a sentence includes a list, contrast, or comparison, the items being listed, contrasted, or compared should have the **same grammatical form**.

Sentence A contains two clauses that contrast teaching in the '70s and '80s with teaching today. However, the comparison is not parallel: the first sentence is in the **active voice**, but the second is in the **passive voice** (Lesson 29). Sentence B reads more smoothly because both clauses are in the active voice, which aligns the subjects and clarifies the contrast.

Sentence C ascribes three adjectives to Ms. Kelly's instructions, but not in a parallel form. Sentence D clarifies the central idea by putting these adjectives in a clear and parallel list.

Lesson 9: Watch for standard parallel constructions

Which is better?

  A. *It seems sometimes that our representatives would rather generate sound bites for their partisans instead of working to solve our social and economic problems.*

  B. *It seems sometimes that our representatives would rather generate sound bites for their partisans than solve our social and economic problems.*

The problem in sentence A is hard for most readers to catch. It may take a few readings before you notice it. The word *rather* indicates that the sentence is making a contrast. Such a contrast requires a **standard parallel construction**: *rather X than Y.* When you see the word *rather*, you should expect the word *than* to appear soon afterward. But in sentence A, not only does *than* not appear, but the two words from *X* and *Y* that should be parallel are not: *generate* is a present-tense verb, but *working* is a gerund. Sentence B makes the correction, and creates the parallel construction *rather generate . . . than solve.*

Use the following **standard parallel constructions** precisely. When you use any of these phrases, use the precise wording, and make sure *X* and *Y* are parallel.

rather X than Y	*X more than Y*	*neither X nor Y*	*X is like Y*
prefer X to Y	*either X or Y*	*both X and Y*	*the more X, the more Y*
less X than Y	*not so much X as Y*	*not X but Y*	*the better X, the better Y*

Lesson 10: Avoid number shifts

If a sentence equates two things, those things should have the **same number**.

Which is better?

A. *Everyone enjoyed their meal.*
B. *Everyone enjoyed his or her meal.*
C. *They all enjoyed their meals.*

Sentence A commits a **number shift**: the pronoun *their* is plural, but its antecedent *everyone* is singular. Additionally, the object *meal* is singular, which doesn't make sense—are multiple people sharing a single meal? One way to correct this problem is by changing *their* to the singular *his or her*, as in sentence B. But this phrase is needlessly awkward. Sentence C avoids both problems, so it is the best of the three.

Consider this sentence:

The problem with this plan is all of the permits we would have to file before starting the project.

If we trim it a bit, we get

The problem ~~with this plan~~ is all of the permits we would have to file ~~before starting the project~~.

Again, we have a number shift: the singular *problem* is equated with the plural *all of the permits*. We could try to fix the problem by pluralizing the subject:

The problems with this plan are all of the permits we would have to file before starting the project.

But that sounds very strange. The best revision strengthens the verb to avoid the number shift:

Filing all of the permits required by this plan will probably delay the project.

The SAT Essay

What is the SAT Essay?

The SAT includes an **optional** 50-minute Essay assignment designed to assess your

> *proficiency in writing a cogent and clear analysis of a challenging rhetorical essay written for a broad audience.*

Should you choose to accept the challenge, the SAT Essay will be the fifth and final section of your test.

The SAT Essay assignment asks you to read a 650–750 word rhetorical essay (such as a *New York Times* op-ed about the economic pros and cons of using biofuels) and to write a well-organized response that

- demonstrates an understanding of the essay's central ideas and important details
- analyzes its use of evidence, such as facts or examples, to support its claims
- critiques its use of reasoning to develop ideas to connect claims and evidence
- examines how it uses stylistic or persuasive elements, such as word choice or appeals to emotion, to add power to the ideas expressed

How is it used?

Many colleges use the SAT Essay in admissions or placement decisions. Many also regard it as an important indicator of essential skills for success in college, specifically, your ability to demonstrate understanding of complex reading assignments, to analyze arguments, and to express your thoughts in writing.

Sound intimidating? It's not.

Strong active reading of the source text is the first and most important step in the analytical writing task. There are four rules to success on the SAT Essay, and the lessons in this chapter will give you the knowledge you need to master them.

Understand the Analytical Task

Lesson 1: Use your 50 minutes wisely

The SAT Essay assesses your proficiency in reading, analysis, and writing. You are given 50 minutes to read an argumentative essay and write an analysis that demonstrates your comprehension of the essay's primary and secondary ideas and your understanding of its use of evidence, language, reasoning, and rhetorical or literary elements to support those ideas. You must support your claims with evidence from the text and use critical reasoning to evaluate its rhetorical effectiveness.

So what should you do with those 50 minutes?

Reading: 15–20 minutes

Although 15–20 minutes may seem like a long time to devote to reading a 750-word essay, remember that you must do more than simply read the essay. You must comprehend the essay and analyze its stylistic and rhetorical elements. In other words, you must master the "Three-Pass Approach" that we will practice in lessons 4–6. This is a fairly advanced reading technique, and you will need to devote substantial time to practicing it. Even once you've mastered it, you will still need to set aside 15–20 minutes on the SAT Essay section to read and annotate the passage thoroughly.

Organizing: 10–15 minutes

Your next task is to gather the ideas from your analyses and use them to formulate a thesis and structure for a five- or six-paragraph essay. If you have performed your first task properly and have completed your "Three-Pass" analysis, creating an outline will be much easier. We will discuss these tasks in lessons 7 and 8.

Your thesis should summarize the thesis of the essay and its secondary ideas, describe the author's main stylistic and rhetorical elements, and explain how these elements support (or detract from) the author's argument.

Take your time with this process, too. Don't start writing before you have articulated a thoughtful guiding question and outlined the essay as a whole.

Writing: 20–25 minutes

Next, of course, you have to write your easy. To get a high score, your essay must provide an eloquent introduction and conclusion, articulate a thesis summarizing the central claims and the main rhetorical and stylistic elements of the essay, be well organized, show a logical and cohesive progression of ideas, maintain a formal style and an objective tone, and show a strong command of language. But if you've followed these steps, which we will explore in more detail below, the essay will flow naturally and easily from your analysis and outline.

Lesson 2: Learn the format of the SAT Essay

> SAT Essay passages are "op-ed" passages that present a point of view on a topic in the arts, sciences, politics, or culture. They address a broad audience, express nuanced views on complex subjects, and use evidence and reasoning to support their claims.
>
> Below is a sample essay and prompt (from the diagnostic test in Chapter 2). Read it carefully to familiarize yourself with the instructions and format.

You have <u>50 minutes</u> to read the passage and write an essay in response to the prompt provided below.

DIRECTIONS

As you read the passage below, consider how Steven Pinker uses

- evidence, such as facts or examples, to support his claims
- reasoning to develop ideas and connect claims and evidence
- stylistic or persuasive elements, such as word choice or appeals to emotion, to add power to the ideas expressed

---

Adapted from Steven Pinker, "Mind Over Mass Media." ©2010 by *The New York Times*. Originally published June 10, 2010.

1   New forms of media have always caused moral panics: the printing press, newspapers, paperbacks and television were all once denounced as threats to their consumers' brainpower and moral fiber.

2   So too with electronic technologies. PowerPoint, we're told, is reducing discourse to bullet points. Search engines lower our intelligence, encouraging us to skim on the surface of knowledge rather than dive to its depths. Twitter is shrinking our attention spans.

3   But such panics often fail reality checks. When comic books were accused of turning juveniles into delinquents in the 1950s, crime was falling to record lows, just as the denunciations of video games in the 1990s coincided with the great American crime decline. The decades of television, transistor radios and rock videos were also decades in which I.Q. scores rose continuously.

4   For a reality check today, take the state of science, which demands high levels of brainwork and is measured by clear benchmarks of discovery. Today, scientists are never far from their e-mail and cannot lecture without PowerPoint. If electronic media were hazardous to intelligence, the quality of science would be plummeting. Yet discoveries are multiplying like fruit flies, and progress is dizzying. Other activities in the life of the mind, like philosophy, history and cultural criticism, are likewise flourishing.

5   Critics of new media sometimes use science itself to press their case, citing research that shows how "experience can change the brain." But cognitive neuroscientists roll their eyes at such talk. Yes, every time we learn a fact or skill the wiring of the brain changes; it's not as if the information is stored in the pancreas. But the existence of neural plasticity does not mean the brain is a blob of clay pounded into shape by experience.

6   Experience does not revamp the basic information-processing capacities of the brain. Speed-reading programs have long claimed to do just that, but the verdict was rendered by Woody Allen after he read *War and Peace* in one sitting: "It was about Russia." Genuine multitasking, too, has been exposed as a myth, not just by laboratory studies but by the familiar sight of an SUV undulating between lanes as the driver cuts deals on his cellphone.

7   Moreover, the evidence indicates that the effects of experience are highly specific to the experiences themselves. If you train people to do one thing, they get better at doing that thing, but almost nothing else. Music doesn't make you better at math; conjugating Latin doesn't make you more logical; brain-training games don't make you smarter. Accomplished people don't bulk up their brains with intellectual calisthenics; they immerse themselves in their fields. Novelists read lots of novels; scientists read lots of science.

8   The effects of consuming electronic media are also likely to be far more limited than the panic implies. Media critics write as if the brain takes on the qualities of whatever it consumes, the informational equivalent of "you are what you eat." As with primitive peoples who believe that eating fierce animals will make them fierce, they assume that watching quick cuts in rock videos turns your mental life into quick cuts or that reading bullet points and Twitter postings turns your thoughts into bullet points and Twitter postings.

9   Yes, the constant arrival of information packets can be distracting or addictive, especially to people with attention deficit disorder. But distraction is not a new phenomenon. The solution is not to bemoan technology but to develop strategies of self-control, as we do with every other temptation in life. Turn off e-mail or Twitter when you work, put away your BlackBerry at dinner time, ask your spouse to call you to bed at a designated hour.

10   And to encourage intellectual depth, don't rail at PowerPoint or Google. It's not as if habits of deep reflection, thorough research and rigorous reasoning ever came naturally to people. They must be acquired in special institutions, which we call universities, and maintained with constant upkeep, which we call analysis, criticism and debate. They are not granted by propping a heavy encyclopedia on your lap, nor are they taken away by efficient access to information on the Internet.

11   The new media have caught on for a reason. Knowledge is increasing exponentially; human brainpower and waking hours are not. Fortunately, the Internet and information technologies are helping us manage, search, and retrieve our collective intellectual output at different scales, from Twitter and previews to e-books and online encyclopedias. Far from making us stupid, these technologies are the only things that will keep us smart.

Write an essay in which you explain how Steven Pinker builds an argument to persuade his audience that new media are not destroying our moral and intellectual abilities. In your essay, analyze how Pinker uses one or more of the features listed in the box above (or features of your own choice) to strengthen the logic and persuasiveness of his argument. Be sure that your analysis focuses on the most relevant features of the passage.

Your essay should NOT explain whether you agree with Pinker's claims, but rather explain how Pinker builds an argument to persuade his audience.

Lesson 3: Understand the scoring rubric

Your essay will be scored based on three criteria: **reading**, **analysis**, and **writing**. Two trained readers will give your essay a score of 1 to 4 on these three criteria, and your subscore for each criterion will be the sum of these two, that is, a score from 2 to 8. Here is the official rubric for all three criteria.

SAT Essay Scoring Rubric

Score	Reading	Analysis	Writing
4	• demonstrates a thorough understanding of the source text, including its central ideas, its important details, and how they interrelate • is free of errors of fact or interpretation with regard to the text • makes skillful use of textual evidence (quotations, paraphrases, or both) to demonstrate a complete understanding of the source text	• offers an insightful analysis of the source text and demonstrates a sophisticated understanding of the analytical task • offers a thorough, well-considered evaluation of the author's use of evidence, reasoning, and/or stylistic and persuasive elements, and/or features of the student's own choosing • contains relevant, sufficient, and strategically chosen support for claims or points made • focuses consistently on those features of the text that are most relevant to addressing the task	• is cohesive and demonstrates a highly effective command of language • includes a precise central claim • includes an eloquent introduction and conclusion, and demonstrates a logical and effective progression of ideas within and among paragraphs • uses an effective variety of sentence structures, demonstrates precise word choice, and maintains a formal style and objective tone • shows a strong command of the conventions of Standard Written English and is free or virtually free of errors
3	• demonstrates effective understanding of the source text, including its central ideas and important details • is free of substantive errors of fact and interpretation with regard to the text • makes appropriate use of textual evidence (quotations, paraphrases, or both) to demonstrate an understanding of the source text	• offers an effective analysis of the source text and demonstrates an understanding of the analytical task • competently evaluates the author's use of evidence, reasoning, and/or stylistic and persuasive elements, and/or features of the student's own choosing • contains relevant and sufficient support for claims or points made • focuses primarily on those features of the text that are most relevant to addressing the task	• is mostly cohesive and demonstrates effective control of language • includes a central claim or implicit controlling idea • includes an effective introduction and conclusion, and demonstrates a clear progression of ideas within and among paragraphs • uses a variety of sentence structures, demonstrates some precise word choice, and maintains a formal style and objective tone • shows a good control of the conventions of Standard Written English and is free of significant errors that detract from the quality of writing

2	• demonstrates some understanding of the source text, including its central ideas, but not of important details • may contain errors of fact and/or interpretation with regard to the text • makes limited and/or haphazard use of textual evidence (quotations, paraphrases, or both) to demonstrate some understanding of the source text	• offers limited analysis of the source text and demonstrates only partial understanding of the analytical task • identifies and attempts to describe the author's use of evidence, reasoning, and/or stylistic and persuasive elements, and/or features of the student's own choosing, but merely asserts rather than explains their importance, or makes unwarranted claims • contains little or no support for claims • may lack a clear focus on those features of the text that are most relevant to addressing the task	• demonstrates little or no cohesion and limited skill in the use and control of language • may lack a clear central claim or controlling idea or may deviate from the claim or idea • lacks an effective introduction and/or conclusion • may demonstrate some progression of ideas within paragraphs but not throughout • has limited variety in sentence structures • demonstrates inconsistently effective diction and deviates noticeably from a formal style and objective tone • shows a limited control of the conventions of Standard Written English and contains errors that detract from the quality of writing and may impede understanding
1	• demonstrates little or no comprehension of the source text • fails to show an understanding of the text's central ideas, and may include only details without reference to central ideas • may contain numerous errors of fact or interpretation with regard to the text • makes little or no use of textual evidence (quotations, paraphrases, or both), demonstrating little or no understanding of the source text	• offers little or no analysis or ineffective analysis of the source text and demonstrates little or no understanding of the analytic task • identifies without explanation some aspects of the author's use of evidence, reasoning, and/or stylistic and persuasive elements • makes unwarranted analytical claims • contains little or no support for claims, or support is largely irrelevant • may not focus on features of the text that are relevant to addressing the task • offers no discernible analysis (e.g., is largely or exclusively summary)	• demonstrates little or no cohesion and inadequate skill in the use and control of language • may lack a clear central claim or controlling idea • lacks a recognizable introduction and conclusion, and lacks any discernible progression of ideas • lacks variety in sentence structures, demonstrates weak diction, and may lack a formal style and objective tone • shows a weak control of the conventions of Standard Written English and may contain numerous errors that undermine the quality of writing

Read the Passage Using the "Three-Pass Approach"

Lesson 4: First pass: Summarize

Use the first 15 to 20 minutes to read the passage thoroughly, using the "three-pass approach" described in these next three lessons. In the first pass, read and summarize the passage as we discussed in Chapter 4, asking, "What is the central thesis, who is the audience, and what is the general structure of the essay?" Underline key points and summarize the passage with annotations.

Let's apply this strategy to the essay from the diagnostic test in Chapter 2. (If you haven't already completed your diagnostic test essay, flip back to Chapter 2 and do it now!)

Adapted from Steven Pinker, "Mind Over Mass Media." ©2010 by *The New York Times*. Originally published June 10, 2010.

First pass: Summarize

1   New forms of media have always caused moral panics: the printing press, newspapers, paperbacks and television were all once denounced as threats to their consumers' brainpower and moral fiber.

People have long worried that media make us dumb and immoral.

2   So too with electronic technologies. PowerPoint, we're told, is reducing discourse to bullet points. Search engines lower our intelligence, encouraging us to skim on the surface of knowledge rather than dive to its depths. Twitter is shrinking our attention spans.

Today, the same is said of PowerPoint, Google, and Twitter.

3   But such panics often fail reality checks. When comic books were accused of turning juveniles into delinquents in the 1950s, crime was falling to record lows, just as the denunciations of video games in the 1990s coincided with the great American crime decline. The decades of television, transistor radios and rock videos were also decades in which I.Q. scores rose continuously.

But sociological evidence refutes those fears, rather than supports them.

4   For a reality check today, take the state of science, which demands high levels of brainwork and is measured by clear benchmarks of discovery. Today, scientists are never far from their e-mail and cannot lecture without PowerPoint. If electronic media were hazardous to intelligence, the quality of science would be plummeting. Yet discoveries are multiplying like fruit flies, and progress is dizzying. Other activities in the life of the mind, like philosophy, history and cultural criticism, are likewise flourishing.

Scientists use the media, yet are as productive as ever.

The same is true with those who work in the humanities.

5   Critics of new media sometimes use science itself to press their case, citing research that shows how "experience can change the brain." But cognitive neuro-scientists roll their eyes at such talk. Yes, every time we learn a fact or skill the wiring of the brain changes; it's not as if the information is stored in the pancreas. But the existence of neural plasticity does not mean the brain is a blob of clay pounded into shape by experience.

The "science" used to bolster these panics is weak, facile, and misleading.

CONTINUE

6   Experience does not revamp the basic information-processing capacities of the brain. Speed-reading programs have long claimed to do just that, but the verdict was rendered by Woody Allen after he read *War and Peace* in one sitting: "It was about Russia." Genuine multitasking, too, has been exposed as a myth, not just by laboratory studies but by the familiar sight of an SUV undulating between lanes as the driver cuts deals on his cell phone.

> New media don't redesign our brains as easily as the critics suggest.

7   Moreover, the evidence indicates that the effects of experience are highly specific to the experiences themselves. If you train people to do one thing, they get better at doing that thing, but almost nothing else. Music doesn't make you better at math; conjugating Latin doesn't make you more logical; brain-training games don't make you smarter. Accomplished people don't bulk up their brains with intellectual calisthenics; they immerse themselves in their fields. Novelists read lots of novels; scientists read lots of science.

> Cognitive changes require very specific training . . .

8   The effects of consuming electronic media are also likely to be far more limited than the panic implies. Media critics write as if the brain takes on the qualities of whatever it consumes, the informational equivalent of "you are what you eat." As with primitive peoples who believe that eating fierce animals will make them fierce, they assume that watching quick cuts in rock videos turns your mental life into quick cuts or that reading bullet points and Twitter postings turns your thoughts into bullet points and Twitter postings.

> . . . so exposure to new media won't change our brains dramatically.

9   Yes, the constant arrival of information packets can be distracting or addictive, especially to people with attention deficit disorder. But distraction is not a new phenomenon. The solution is not to bemoan technology but to develop strategies of self-control, as we do with every other temptation in life. Turn off e-mail or Twitter when you work, put away your BlackBerry at dinner time, ask your spouse to call you to bed at a designated hour.

> Instantaneous social media can be distracting, so just turn them off when you need to.

10   And to encourage intellectual depth, don't rail at PowerPoint or Google. It's not as if habits of deep reflection, thorough research and rigorous reasoning ever came naturally to people. They must be acquired in special institutions, which we call universities, and maintained with constant upkeep, which we call analysis, criticism and debate. They are not granted by propping a heavy encyclopedia on your lap, nor are they taken away by efficient access to information on the Internet.

> Deep intellectual skills are not eroded by quick access to information, but rather are acquired by practicing the skills of analysis, criticism, and debate.

11   The new media have caught on for a reason. Knowledge is increasing exponentially; human brainpower and waking hours are not. Fortunately, the Internet and information technologies are helping us manage, search, and retrieve our collective intellectual output at different scales, from Twitter and previews to e-books and online encyclopedias. Far from making us stupid, these technologies are the only things that will keep us smart.

> Quick access to information is good.

Lesson 5: Second pass: Analyze

> Now read the passage again, focusing on the **specific rhetorical and stylistic devices** that the author uses to support his or her argument. In particular, note how the author uses evidence, reasoning, appeals to values and emotions, and literary elements to support his or her claims. Pay attention to the five categories or rhetorical elements: **logos**, **pathos**, **ethos**, **mythos**, and **poetics**.

Logos—how a writer uses **reasoning** and **evidence** to support claims.

- *What kind of **reasoning** does the author use to support claims?*

  - <u>Dialectical reasoning</u>: Examining two sides of an issue objectively (the *thesis* and the *antithesis*) and arriving at a *synthesis* that resolves problems with each position.

  - <u>Deductive reasoning</u>: Showing that the claim follows from first principles.

  - <u>Inductive reasoning</u>: Showing that the claim follows a pattern of examples.

- *What kind of **evidence** does the author use to support claims?*

  - <u>Anecdotal evidence</u>: Using personal stories to support a claim.

  - <u>Empirical evidence</u>: Using studies, polls, or objective facts to support a claim.

  - <u>Historical evidence</u>: Showing how the claim fits within a context of historical events.

- *Does the author commit any of these common **logical fallacies**?*

  - <u>Straw man fallacy</u>: Misrepresenting an opposing viewpoint to make it easier to attack. (E.g., *If you support background checks for gun purchases, then you want to take away my right to protect my family!*)

  - <u>Overgeneralization fallacy</u>: Applying an idea beyond the situations in which it is appropriate. (E.g. *Cutting taxes helped the economy during the last recession, so it will help boost the economy now that corporate profits are at a record high!*)

  - <u>Ad hominem fallacy</u>: Attacking the person rather than the person's argument. (E.g., *You don't have a Ph.D., so why should I believe you?*)

  - <u>Consensus or authority fallacy</u>: Suggesting that something is true simply because many people believe it, or because a famous or reputable person or institution claims that it is true. (E.g., *If everyone believes it, it must be true; If Einstein said it, it must be true.*)

  - <u>Correlation for causation fallacy</u>: Suggesting that one thing causes another simply because the two are correlated. (E.g., *Rich people get higher SAT scores, therefore the SAT only measures how rich you are.*)

  - <u>Slippery slope fallacy</u>: Suggesting that one cannot set a standard along a continuum. (E.g., *If we lower the drinking age to 18, what will prevent us from lowering it to 3?*)

Pathos—how a writer appeals to the reader's **emotions** and self-interest

- *What kind of **tone** and **attitude** does the author adopt?*

  - <u>Authoritative/Didactic</u>: Assuming an objective and professorial stance.

  - <u>Conversational</u>: Speaking to the reader as a friend, or as an engaging storyteller.

  - <u>Alarmist</u>: Representing a problem as dire and urgent.

- *Does the author choose words to evoke particular **emotions** in the reader, such as **nostalgia**, **lightheartedness**, **sympathy**, or **anger**?*

Ethos—how a writer establishes **credibility** and appeals to common **values**

- *Does the writer establish his or her **authority** to speak on this topic?*

  - <u>Bona fides:</u> Indicating professional experience or academic qualifications.

  - <u>First person engagement:</u> Revealing personal experience with the topic at hand.

  - <u>Substantive authority:</u> Demonstrating expertise through the details and analytical quality of the writing.

- *What specific **values** does the author appeal to, either explicitly or implicitly?*

Safety	Strength	Economic growth	Education
Competence	Hard work	Morality	Beauty
Nostalgia	National strength	Environmentalism	Creativity

- *Does the writer's thesis serve his or her **self-interest**?*

  - If a professional taxi driver were to argue for banning self-driving taxis, for example, the clear self-interest in the matter would undercut his or her credibility. Arguing against one's self-interest, on the other hand, enhances one's **ethos**.

Mythos—how a writer uses **elements of story** to enhance his or her argument

- *Does the writer **characterize** any person or group according to a conventional **archetype**?*

Hero	Regular guy/gal	Villain	Rebel
Victim	Nurturer	Creator	Jester

- *Does the writer use literary elements such as **irony**, **allusion**, **anthropomorphism**, or **allegory**?*

Poetics—how a writer uses **stylistic elements** to enhance his or her argument

- *Does the writer use of any of these **stylistic devices** to support claims?*

Metaphor	Aphorism	Dysphemism	Analogy
Hyperbole	Parallelism	Imagery	Euphemism

This list is by no means exhaustive, but it provides a solid framework for analyzing the passage. In your second read-through, keep it simple. Just underline the sentences or phrases that use these devices, and categorize the devices in the margin.

Read the annotations in the sample analysis that follows and see how each underlined portion represents that particular device. Train yourself to see these devices in all of the rhetorical essays you read: newspaper op-eds, long form essays, and even your own papers.

This analysis is a critical step in writing the SAT Essay. As the scoring rubric indicates, your essay should *offer a thorough, well-considered evaluation of the author's use of evidence, reasoning, and/or stylistic and persuasive elements.*

The rubric also indicates that a good essay will contain *relevant, sufficient, and strategically chosen support for claims or points made.* This means you must **give quotations from the text that show where the author uses these particular devices and stylistic elements.**

Adapted from Steven Pinker, "Mind Over Mass Media." ©2010 by *The New York Times*. Originally published June 10, 2010.

Second pass: Analyze

1   New forms of media have always caused moral panics: the printing press, newspapers, paperbacks and television were all once denounced as threats to their consumers' brainpower and moral fiber.

— examples for historical context

2   So too with electronic technologies. PowerPoint, we're told, is reducing discourse to bullet points. Search engines lower our intelligence, encouraging us to skim on the surface of knowledge rather than dive to its depths. Twitter is shrinking our attention spans.

— strong verbs

3   But such panics often fail reality checks. When comic books were accused of turning juveniles into delinquents in the 1950s, crime was falling to record lows, just as the denunciations of video games in the 1990s coincided with the great American crime decline. The decades of television, transistor radios and rock videos were also decades in which I.Q. scores rose continuously.

— historical evidence as counterpoint

4   For a reality check today, take the state of science, which demands high levels of brainwork and is measured by clear benchmarks of discovery. Today, scientists are never far from their e-mail and cannot lecture without PowerPoint. If electronic media were hazardous to intelligence, the quality of science would be plummeting. Yet discoveries are multiplying like fruit flies, and progress is dizzying. Other activities in the life of the mind, like philosophy, history and cultural criticism, are likewise flourishing.

— conversational language
— appeal to authority?
— counterexample
— clever simile

5   Critics of new media sometimes use science itself to press their case, citing research that shows how "experience can change the brain." But cognitive neuroscientists roll their eyes at such talk. Yes, every time we learn a fact or skill the wiring of the brain changes; it's not as if the information is stored in the pancreas. But the existence of neural plasticity does not mean the brain is a blob of clay pounded into shape by experience.

— qualification
— sarcasm
— metaphor

6   Experience does not revamp the basic information-processing capacities of the brain. Speed-reading programs have long claimed to do just that, but the verdict was rendered by Woody Allen after he read *War and Peace* in one sitting: "It was about Russia." Genuine multitasking, too, has been exposed as a myth, not just by laboratory studies but by the familiar sight of an SUV undulating between lanes as the driver cuts deals on his cell phone.

— humorous cultural allusion
— counterexample

7   Moreover, the evidence indicates that the effects of experience are highly specific to the experiences themselves. If you train people to do one thing, they get better at doing that thing, but almost nothing else. Music doesn't make you better at math; conjugating Latin doesn't make you more logical; brain-training games don't make you smarter. Accomplished people don't bulk up their brains with intellectual calisthenics;

— didacticism
— examples/analogies

CONTINUE ▶

they immerse themselves in their fields. Novelists read lots of novels; scientists read lots of science.

8   The effects of consuming electronic media are also likely to be far more limited than the panic implies. Media critics write as if the brain takes on the qualities of whatever it consumes, the informational equivalent of "you are what you eat." As with primitive peoples who believe that eating fierce animals will make them fierce, they assume that watching quick cuts in rock videos turns your mental life into quick cuts or that reading bullet points and Twitter postings turns your thoughts into bullet points and Twitter postings.

9   Yes, the constant arrival of information packets can be distracting or addictive, especially to people with attention deficit disorder. But distraction is not a new phenomenon. The solution is not to bemoan technology but to develop strategies of self-control, as we do with every other temptation in life. Turn off e-mail or Twitter when you work, put away your BlackBerry at dinner time, ask your spouse to call you to bed at a designated hour.

10   And to encourage intellectual depth, don't rail at PowerPoint or Google. It's not as if habits of deep reflection, thorough research and rigorous reasoning ever came naturally to people. They must be acquired in special institutions, which we call universities, and maintained with constant upkeep, which we call analysis, criticism and debate. They are not granted by propping a heavy encyclopedia on your lap, nor are they taken away by efficient access to information on the Internet.

11   The new media have caught on for a reason. Knowledge is increasing exponentially; human brainpower and waking hours are not. Fortunately, the Internet and information technologies are helping us manage, search, and retrieve our collective intellectual output at different scales, from Twitter and previews to e-books and online encyclopedias. Far from making us stupid, these technologies are the only things that will keep us smart.

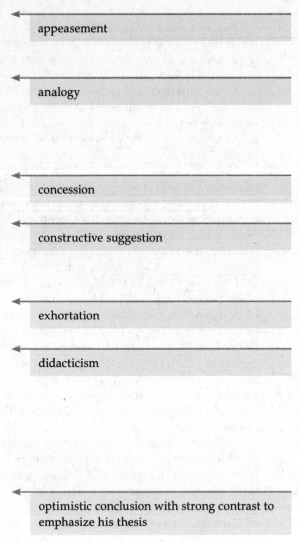

appeasement

analogy

concession

constructive suggestion

exhortation

didacticism

optimistic conclusion with strong contrast to emphasize his thesis

Lesson 6: Third pass: Select and synthesize

In the third pass, read through the annotated passage again and ask: What are the **three or four** rhetorical or stylistic elements that contribute **most significantly** to the writer's argument, and to setting the tone of the passage as a whole? Annotate the passage with this question in mind, and indicate the important examples of these elements in the text.

Adapted from Steven Pinker, "Mind Over Mass Media." ©2010 by *The New York Times*. Originally published June 10, 2010.

Third pass: Select and synthesize

1   New forms of media have always caused moral panics: the printing press, newspapers, paperbacks and television were all once denounced as threats to their consumers' brainpower and moral fiber.

Pinker's reasoning begins by putting an issue in historical context.

2   So too with electronic technologies. PowerPoint, we're told, is reducing discourse to bullet points. Search engines lower our intelligence, encouraging us to skim on the surface of knowledge rather than dive to its depths. Twitter is shrinking our attention spans.

He illustrates the misconception using strong, vivid verbs like "skim," "dive," and "shrink."

3   But such panics often fail reality checks. When comic books were accused of turning juveniles into delinquents in the 1950s, crime was falling to record lows, just as the denunciations of video games in the 1990s coincided with the great American crime decline. The decades of television, transistor radios and rock videos were also decades in which I.Q. scores rose continuously.

He cites historical examples that contradict the popular conception.

4   For a reality check today, take the state of science, which demands high levels of brainwork and is measured by clear benchmarks of discovery. Today, scientists are never far from their e-mail and cannot lecture without PowerPoint. If electronic media were hazardous to intelligence, the quality of science would be plummeting. Yet discoveries are multiplying like fruit flies, and progress is dizzying. Other activities in the life of the mind, like philosophy, history and cultural criticism, are likewise flourishing.

He employs logical analysis by identifying a counterexample to a claim.

Pinker injects humor, since fruit flies are common subjects of genetic studies.

5   Critics of new media sometimes use science itself to press their case, citing research that shows how "experience can change the brain." But cognitive neuroscientists roll their eyes at such talk. Yes, every time we learn a fact or skill the wiring of the brain changes; it's not as if the information is stored in the pancreas. But the existence of neural plasticity does not mean the brain is a blob of clay pounded into shape by experience.

He analyzes the grounds of the counter-argument, but may be oversimplifying that counterargument.

Pinker's attempt at humor might be considered a straw man fallacy.

6   Experience does not revamp the basic information-processing capacities of the brain. Speed-reading programs have long claimed to do just that, but the verdict was rendered by Woody Allen after he read *War and Peace* in one sitting: "It was about Russia." Genuine multitasking, too, has been exposed as a myth, not just

He uses another strong metaphor to illustrate the general misconception.

Pinker uses humor to illustrate a point about the limitations of the brain.

by laboratory studies but by the familiar sight of <u>an SUV undulating between lanes as the driver cuts deals on his cell phone.</u>

7   Moreover, the evidence indicates that the effects of experience are highly specific to the experiences themselves. If you train people to do one thing, they get better at doing that thing, but almost nothing else. <u>Music doesn't make you better at math; conjugating Latin doesn't make you more logical; brain-training games don't make you smarter.</u> Accomplished people don't bulk up their brains with intellectual calisthenics; they immerse themselves in their fields. Novelists read lots of novels; scientists read lots of science.

8   The effects of consuming electronic media are also likely to be far more limited than the panic implies. <u>Media critics write as if the brain takes on the qualities of whatever it consumes, the informational equivalent of "you are what you eat."</u> As with primitive peoples who believe that eating fierce animals will make them fierce, they assume that watching quick cuts in rock videos turns your mental life into quick cuts or that reading bullet points and Twitter postings turns your thoughts into bullet points and Twitter postings.

9   Yes, <u>the constant arrival of information packets can be distracting or addictive, especially to people with attention deficit disorder.</u> But distraction is not a new phenomenon. <u>The solution is not to bemoan technology but to develop strategies of self-control</u>, as we do with every other temptation in life. Turn off e-mail or Twitter when you work, put away your BlackBerry at dinner time, ask your spouse to call you to bed at a designated hour.

10   <u>And to encourage intellectual depth</u>, don't rail at PowerPoint or Google. It's not as if habits of deep reflection, thorough research and rigorous reasoning ever came naturally to people. <u>They must be acquired in special institutions, which we call universities, and maintained with constant upkeep, which we call analysis, criticism and debate.</u> They are not granted by propping a heavy encyclopedia on your lap, nor are they taken away by efficient access to information on the Internet.

11   The new media have caught on for a reason. Knowledge is increasing exponentially; human brainpower and waking hours are not. Fortunately, the Internet and information technologies are helping us manage, search, and retrieve our collective intellectual output at different scales, from Twitter and previews to e-books and online encyclopedias. <u>Far from making us stupid, these technologies are the only things that will keep us smart.</u>

Pinker uses a vivid illustration of the SUV driver to evoke anger (pathos) against those who disagree with him.

Pinker argues by assertion, making intriguing claims, but providing little reasoning or evidence to support them.

Pinker uses an interesting and vivid example, as well as an analogy to a popular proverb, to illustrate a mistaken way of thinking.

Pinker makes an important concession to the opposing view.

He suggests a practical and reasonable solution to the problem.

Pinker appeals to the value of "intellectual depth" (ethos), and provides a more detailed solution to the problem.

He adopts a didactic tone here, arguing by assertion and admonition.

Pinker concludes with a stark contrast to emphasize his thesis.

Write the Essay

Lesson 7: Write with strong verbs and concrete nouns

Now you should have between 20 and 25 minutes left, which should be plenty of time to write your essay on the official essay sheets. As you write, keep the following points in mind in order to get a high score in the "writing" category.

Minimize weak verbs by upgrading "lurkers"

Look at a recent essay you've written and circle all of the verbs. Are more than one-third of your verbs *to be* verbs (*is, are, was, were*)? If so, strengthen your verbs. You cannot maintain a strong discussion if you overuse weak verbs like *to be*, *to have*, and *to do*.

> To strengthen your sentences, upgrade any **lurkers**—the words in your sentence that aren't verbs, but should be. Consider this sentence:
>
> > This action **is** *in violation of our company's confidentiality policy.*
>
> It revolves around a very weak verb. But the noun *violation* is a lurker. Let's upgrade it to verb status:
>
> > This action **violates** *our company's confidentiality policy.*
>
> Notice how this small change "punches up" the sentence.

Here are some more examples of how upgrading the lurkers can strengthen a sentence:

Weak: *My failure on the test **was** reflective of the fact of my not having studied.*

Stronger: *I **failed** the test because I **didn't study**.*

Here, we've upgraded the lurkers *reflective* (adjective) and *having studied* (participle). Notice that this change not only strengthens the verbs and clarifies the sentence, but also unclutters the sentence by eliminating the prepositional phrases *on the test*, *of the fact*, and *of my not having studied*.

Weak: *The fact of the governor's ignoring the protestors **made** them resentful of him.*

Stronger: *The protestors **resented** the fact that the governor **ignored** them.*

We've upgraded the lurkers *ignoring* (gerund) and *resentful* (adjective). Again, notice that strengthening the sentence also unclutters it of unnecessary prepositional phrases.

Weak: *The mice **had** a tendency to overeat when they **had** a lack of this hormone.*

Stronger: *The mice **overate** when they **lacked** this hormone.*

We've upgraded the lurkers *to overeat* (infinitive) and *lack* (noun).

Activate your passive verbs

> What is the difference between these two sentences?

> *The rebel army made its bold maneuver under the cloak of darkness.*
>
> *The bold maneuver was made by the rebel army under the cloak of darkness.*

These two sentences say essentially the same thing, but the first sentence is in the **active voice** whereas the second is in the **passive voice**. In the **active voice**, the subject of the sentence is the "actor" of the verb, but in the **passive voice**, the subject is *not* the actor. (The *maneuver* did not *make* anything, so *maneuver* is not the *actor* of the verb *made* in the second sentence, even though it is the subject.) Notice that the second sentence is weaker for two reasons: it's heavier (it has more words) *and* it's slower (it takes more time to get to the point).

But there's an even better reason to avoid passive voice verbs: they can make you sound deceitful. Consider this classic passive-voice sentence:

> *Mistakes were made.*

Who made them? Thanks to the passive voice, we don't need to say. We can avoid responsibility.

Although you may sometimes need to use the **passive voice**, avoid it when you can. The **active voice** is clearer and stronger, and it encourages you to articulate essential details (like "who did it") for your reader.

Weak: *The entire project **was completed by** Joe in less than a week.*

Stronger: *Joe **completed** the entire project in less than a week.*

Use concrete and personal nouns

Clarify and strengthen your sentences by using **concrete nouns** (nouns that signify things that we can see, hear, or touch) and **personal nouns and pronouns** (like *we, us, people, humans, anyone*, and so on). Abstract nouns (like *consideration, belief, ability*, and *information*) are harder for readers to grasp than concrete and personal nouns.

When we strengthen our verbs, our nouns often become more concrete and personal automatically:

Weak: *My **failure** on the **test** was reflective of the **fact** of my not **having studied**.*

Stronger: *I failed the **test** because I didn't study.*

In the first sentence, 75% of the nouns (*failure, fact*, and *having studied*) are abstract, but in the second, the nouns and pronouns (*I, test, I*) are personal and concrete. Notice that the second sentence is clearer, more concise, and more effective.

Weak: *The **fact** of the governor's **ignoring** the **protestors** made **them** resentful of **him**.*

Stronger: *The **protestors** resented the **fact** that the **governor** ignored **them**.*

By upgrading the gerund *ignoring* to a verb, we reduced the number of abstract nouns in the sentence by 50%. Even better, we upgraded the subject from an abstract noun (*fact*) to a concrete and personal one (*protestors*). The second sentence is simpler, clearer, and stronger.

Lesson 8: Create a logical flow of ideas

The official SAT Essay scoring rubric says that a strong essay must *demonstrate a logical and effective progression of ideas*. Therefore, make sure your essay **explains** each of your ideas clearly, and **connects** each idea to one of your central claims.

Explain your ideas

Don't merely state your ideas: *explain* them clearly enough so that your reader can easily follow your analysis.

Weak: *Pinker attempts to refute his critics with analogy.*

Stronger: *Pinker attempts to refute cultural critics by drawing an analogy between their reasoning and the faulty reasoning of "primitive peoples" who believe that "eating fierce animals will make them fierce."*

Good explanations often include words like **by** (*our team slowed down the game by using a full-court press*), **because** (*we won because we executed our game plan flawlessly*), or **therefore** (*we slowed down their offense; therefore, we were able to manage the game more effectively*).

Be careful, however, of overusing using phrases like **because of** and **due to**. These phrases tend to produce weak explanations because they link to *noun phrases* rather than *clauses*. Clauses are more explanatory because they include verbs and therefore convey more information.

Weak: *The essay works **because of** its imagery.*

Stronger: *The essay works **because** its images evoke powerful ideas that support the thesis.*

Notice that avoiding the *of* forces the writer to provide a *clause* instead of just a *noun phrase* and therefore give a more substantial explanation.

Connect your ideas with clear cross-references

Strong analytical essays should provide clear **cross-references** in order to connect ideas and establish a clear chain of reasoning. One way to clarify your chain of reasoning is by **using your pronouns carefully**, particularly when they refer to ideas mentioned in previous sentences. Make sure your pronouns have clear antecedents.

Consider these sentences:

Davis makes the important point that defense lawyers sometimes must represent clients whom they know are guilty, not only because these lawyers take an oath to uphold their clients' right to an adequate defense, but also because firms cannot survive financially if they accept only the obviously innocent as clients. This troubles many who want to pursue criminal law.

What does the pronoun *This* in the second sentence refer to? What *troubles many who want to study criminal law*? Is it the fact that Davis is making this point? Is it the moral implications of lawyers representing the guilty? Is it the technical difficulty of lawyers representing the guilty? Is it the financial challenges of maintaining a viable law practice? Is it all of these? The ambiguity of this pronoun obscures the discussion and makes the reader work harder to follow it. Clarify your references so that your train of thought is easy to follow.

*Davis makes the important point that defense lawyers sometimes must represent clients whom they know are guilty, not only because these lawyers take an oath to uphold their clients' right to an adequate defense, but also because firms cannot survive financially if they accept only the obviously innocent as clients. **Such moral and financial dilemmas** trouble many who want to pursue criminal law.*

Connect your ideas with logical transitions

As you move from idea to idea—within a sentence, between sentences, or between paragraphs—always consider the logical relationship between these ideas, and make these connections clear to your reader. The logical "connectors" include words and phrases like

for example	*furthermore*
moreover	*alternatively*
therefore	*however*
first, second, third	*otherwise*
because	*although*
nevertheless	*subsequently*
commensurately	*hence*
thereby	*as a consequence*

Structure each sentence to fit its purpose

According to the official SAT Essay scoring rubric, a strong essay *uses an effective variety of sentence structures.* Short sentences have impact; long sentences have weight. Good writers vary the structure of their sentences to fit the purpose of that particular discussion.

Consider this paragraph:

Medical interns are overworked. They are constantly asked to do a lot with very little sleep. They are chronically exhausted as a result. They can make mistakes that are dangerous and even potentially deadly.

What is so clumsy about these sentences? They all have the same structure. Consider this revision:

Constantly overworked and given very little time to sleep, medical interns are chronically exhausted. These conditions can lead them to make dangerous and even deadly mistakes.

Your readers won't appreciate your profound ideas if your sentences are poorly constructed. Now consider these sentences:

Gun advocates tell us that "guns don't kill people; people kill people." On the surface, this statement seems obviously true. However, analysis of the assumptions and implications of this statement shows clearly that even its most ardent believers can't possibly believe it.

Now consider this alternative:

Gun advocates tell us that "guns don't kill people; people kill people." On the surface, this statement seems obviously true. It's not.

Which is better? The first provides more information, but the second provides more impact. Good writers always think about the length of their sentences. Long sentences are often necessary for articulating complex ideas, but short sentences are better for emphasizing important points. Choose wisely.

PART IV

SAT Practice Test

ANSWER SHEET for PRACTICE TEST

Use a No. 2 pencil and fill in the entire circle darkly and completely.
If you change your response, erase as completely as possible

SECTION 1

1 Ⓐ Ⓑ Ⓒ Ⓓ	13 Ⓐ Ⓑ Ⓒ Ⓓ	25 Ⓐ Ⓑ Ⓒ Ⓓ	37 Ⓐ Ⓑ Ⓒ Ⓓ	49 Ⓐ Ⓑ Ⓒ Ⓓ
2 Ⓐ Ⓑ Ⓒ Ⓓ	14 Ⓐ Ⓑ Ⓒ Ⓓ	26 Ⓐ Ⓑ Ⓒ Ⓓ	38 Ⓐ Ⓑ Ⓒ Ⓓ	50 Ⓐ Ⓑ Ⓒ Ⓓ
3 Ⓐ Ⓑ Ⓒ Ⓓ	15 Ⓐ Ⓑ Ⓒ Ⓓ	27 Ⓐ Ⓑ Ⓒ Ⓓ	39 Ⓐ Ⓑ Ⓒ Ⓓ	51 Ⓐ Ⓑ Ⓒ Ⓓ
4 Ⓐ Ⓑ Ⓒ Ⓓ	16 Ⓐ Ⓑ Ⓒ Ⓓ	28 Ⓐ Ⓑ Ⓒ Ⓓ	40 Ⓐ Ⓑ Ⓒ Ⓓ	52 Ⓐ Ⓑ Ⓒ Ⓓ
5 Ⓐ Ⓑ Ⓒ Ⓓ	17 Ⓐ Ⓑ Ⓒ Ⓓ	29 Ⓐ Ⓑ Ⓒ Ⓓ	41 Ⓐ Ⓑ Ⓒ Ⓓ	
6 Ⓐ Ⓑ Ⓒ Ⓓ	18 Ⓐ Ⓑ Ⓒ Ⓓ	30 Ⓐ Ⓑ Ⓒ Ⓓ	42 Ⓐ Ⓑ Ⓒ Ⓓ	
7 Ⓐ Ⓑ Ⓒ Ⓓ	19 Ⓐ Ⓑ Ⓒ Ⓓ	31 Ⓐ Ⓑ Ⓒ Ⓓ	43 Ⓐ Ⓑ Ⓒ Ⓓ	
8 Ⓐ Ⓑ Ⓒ Ⓓ	20 Ⓐ Ⓑ Ⓒ Ⓓ	32 Ⓐ Ⓑ Ⓒ Ⓓ	44 Ⓐ Ⓑ Ⓒ Ⓓ	
9 Ⓐ Ⓑ Ⓒ Ⓓ	21 Ⓐ Ⓑ Ⓒ Ⓓ	33 Ⓐ Ⓑ Ⓒ Ⓓ	45 Ⓐ Ⓑ Ⓒ Ⓓ	
10 Ⓐ Ⓑ Ⓒ Ⓓ	22 Ⓐ Ⓑ Ⓒ Ⓓ	34 Ⓐ Ⓑ Ⓒ Ⓓ	46 Ⓐ Ⓑ Ⓒ Ⓓ	
11 Ⓐ Ⓑ Ⓒ Ⓓ	23 Ⓐ Ⓑ Ⓒ Ⓓ	35 Ⓐ Ⓑ Ⓒ Ⓓ	47 Ⓐ Ⓑ Ⓒ Ⓓ	
12 Ⓐ Ⓑ Ⓒ Ⓓ	24 Ⓐ Ⓑ Ⓒ Ⓓ	36 Ⓐ Ⓑ Ⓒ Ⓓ	48 Ⓐ Ⓑ Ⓒ Ⓓ	

SECTION 2

1 Ⓐ Ⓑ Ⓒ Ⓓ	11 Ⓐ Ⓑ Ⓒ Ⓓ	21 Ⓐ Ⓑ Ⓒ Ⓓ	31 Ⓐ Ⓑ Ⓒ Ⓓ	41 Ⓐ Ⓑ Ⓒ Ⓓ
2 Ⓐ Ⓑ Ⓒ Ⓓ	12 Ⓐ Ⓑ Ⓒ Ⓓ	22 Ⓐ Ⓑ Ⓒ Ⓓ	32 Ⓐ Ⓑ Ⓒ Ⓓ	42 Ⓐ Ⓑ Ⓒ Ⓓ
3 Ⓐ Ⓑ Ⓒ Ⓓ	13 Ⓐ Ⓑ Ⓒ Ⓓ	23 Ⓐ Ⓑ Ⓒ Ⓓ	33 Ⓐ Ⓑ Ⓒ Ⓓ	43 Ⓐ Ⓑ Ⓒ Ⓓ
4 Ⓐ Ⓑ Ⓒ Ⓓ	14 Ⓐ Ⓑ Ⓒ Ⓓ	24 Ⓐ Ⓑ Ⓒ Ⓓ	34 Ⓐ Ⓑ Ⓒ Ⓓ	44 Ⓐ Ⓑ Ⓒ Ⓓ
5 Ⓐ Ⓑ Ⓒ Ⓓ	15 Ⓐ Ⓑ Ⓒ Ⓓ	25 Ⓐ Ⓑ Ⓒ Ⓓ	35 Ⓐ Ⓑ Ⓒ Ⓓ	
6 Ⓐ Ⓑ Ⓒ Ⓓ	16 Ⓐ Ⓑ Ⓒ Ⓓ	26 Ⓐ Ⓑ Ⓒ Ⓓ	36 Ⓐ Ⓑ Ⓒ Ⓓ	
7 Ⓐ Ⓑ Ⓒ Ⓓ	17 Ⓐ Ⓑ Ⓒ Ⓓ	27 Ⓐ Ⓑ Ⓒ Ⓓ	37 Ⓐ Ⓑ Ⓒ Ⓓ	
8 Ⓐ Ⓑ Ⓒ Ⓓ	18 Ⓐ Ⓑ Ⓒ Ⓓ	28 Ⓐ Ⓑ Ⓒ Ⓓ	38 Ⓐ Ⓑ Ⓒ Ⓓ	
9 Ⓐ Ⓑ Ⓒ Ⓓ	19 Ⓐ Ⓑ Ⓒ Ⓓ	29 Ⓐ Ⓑ Ⓒ Ⓓ	39 Ⓐ Ⓑ Ⓒ Ⓓ	
10 Ⓐ Ⓑ Ⓒ Ⓓ	20 Ⓐ Ⓑ Ⓒ Ⓓ	30 Ⓐ Ⓑ Ⓒ Ⓓ	40 Ⓐ Ⓑ Ⓒ Ⓓ	

BEGIN YOUR ESSAY HERE

DO NOT WRITE OUTSIDE OF THE BOX.

Cut Here

1

1

Reading Practice Test

65 MINUTES, 52 QUESTIONS

Turn to Section 1 of your answer sheet to answer the questions in this section.

DIRECTIONS

Each passage or pair of passages below is followed by a number of questions. After reading each passage or pair, choose the best answer to each question based on what is stated or implied in the passage or passages and in any accompanying graphics.

Questions 1–10 are based on the following passage.

This passage is from Ralph Waldo Emerson, *"Prudence."* Public domain. First published in 1841.

What right have I to write on prudence, of which I have little, and that of the negative sort?
Line My prudence consists in avoiding and going without, not in the inventing of means and
5 methods, not in adroit steering, not in gentle repairing. I have no skill to make money spend well, no genius in my economy, and whoever sees my garden discovers that I must have some other garden. Yet I love facts, and hate shiftiness and
10 people without perception.

Then I have the same title to write on prudence that I have to write on poetry or holiness. We write from aspiration as well as from experience.
15 We paint those qualities that we do not possess. The poet admires the man of energy and tactics; the merchant breeds his son for the church or the bar; and where a man is not vain and egotistic you shall find what he lacks, by his praise.
20 Yet it would be hardly honest for me not to balance these fine lyric words with words of coarser sound. Prudence is the virtue of the senses. It is the science of appearances. It is the outmost action of the inward life. It is God taking
25 thought for oxen. It moves matter after the laws of matter. It is content to seek health of body by

complying with physical conditions, and health of mind by the laws of the intellect.

The world of the senses is a world of shows;
30 it does not exist for itself, but has a symbolic character; and a true prudence or law of shows recognizes the co-presence of other laws and knows that its own office is secondary; knows that it is surface and not center where it works.
35 Prudence is false when detached. It is legitimate when it is the natural history of the soul incarnate, when it unfolds the beauty of laws within the narrow scope of the senses.

There are all degrees of proficiency in
40 knowledge of the world. It is sufficient to our present purpose to indicate three. One class lives to the utility of the symbol, esteeming health and wealth a final good. Another class lives above this mark, to the beauty of the symbol, as the poet and
45 artist and the naturalist and man of science. A third class lives above the beauty of the symbol to the beauty of the thing signified; these are wise men. The first class has common sense; the second, taste; and the third, spiritual perception.
50 Once in a long time, a man traverses the whole scale, and sees and enjoys the symbol solidly, then also has a clear eye for its beauty, and lastly, while he pitches his tent on this sacred volcanic isle of nature, does not offer to build houses and barns
55 thereon, reverencing the splendor of the God which he sees bursting through each chink and cranny.

CONTINUE ▶

1 | **1**

The world is filled with the proverbs and
acts of a base prudence, which is a devotion to
60 matter, as if we possessed no other faculties than
the palate, the nose, the touch, the eye and ear; a
prudence that never subscribes, that never gives,
that seldom lends, and asks but one question of
any project: will it bake bread? This is a disease
65 like a thickening of the skin until the vital organs
are destroyed. But culture, revealing the high
origin of the apparent world and aiming at the
perfection of the man as the end, degrades every
thing else, as health and bodily life, into means.
70 It sees prudence not to be a separate faculty, but
a name for wisdom and virtue conversing with
the body and its wants. Cultivated men always
feel and speak so, as if a great fortune, the
achievement of a civil or social measure, great
75 personal influence, a graceful and commanding
address, had their value as proofs of the energy of
the spirit. If a man loses his balance and immerses
himself in any trades or pleasures for their own
sake, he may be a good wheel or pin, but he is not
80 a cultivated man.

1

The tone of the first paragraph is best described as

A) self-effacing.
B) pontifical.
C) aspirational.
D) sardonic.

2

The author's reference to "some other garden" (lines
8–9) primarily suggests that he

A) finds solace in the art of planting.
B) seeks new challenges and experiences.
C) considers arable land to be a valuable resource.
D) lacks the particular skills associated with
farming.

3

In line 11, "title" most nearly means

A) ownership.
B) office.
C) authority.
D) publication.

4

The author believes that he is justified in acting as
an authority on prudence primarily because of his

A) experience in making decisions.
B) regret for his past mistakes.
C) studies in classical philosophy.
D) yearning for wisdom.

5

Which choice provides the strongest evidence for
the answer to the previous question?

A) Lines 6–9 ("I have no skill . . . some other
garden")
B) Lines 13–14 ("We write from . . . as well as from
experience")
C) Lines 20–22 ("Yet it would . . . coarser sound")
D) Lines 26–28 ("It is content . . . laws of the
intellect")

6

The passage suggests that members of the "third class" (line 46) are superior for their ability to

A) solve important problems.

B) discern sublime qualities.

C) create works of beauty.

D) reason logically.

7

The "houses and barns" (line 54) represent

A) an unwise allegiance to worldly things.

B) the rejection of mere symbols.

C) the nobility of living with nature.

D) the importance of strong belief.

8

In line 59, "base" most nearly means

A) supportive.

B) ignoble.

C) necessary.

D) straightforward.

9

The "disease" mentioned in line 64 is best described as

A) apathy.

B) gluttony.

C) sensuousness.

D) egotism.

10

The passage as a whole characterizes prudence primarily as

A) the aspiration to wisdom and righteousness.

B) a commitment to aesthetic principles.

C) the pursuit of practical skills and sensory experience.

D) the noble pursuit of spiritual goals.

CONTINUE

1   1

Questions 11–21 are based on the following passage.

This passage is from Joseph Conrad, *The Secret Sharer*. It was originally published in 1912. The narrator of this story is the captain of a ship about to begin a voyage.

She floated at the starting point of a long journey, very still in an immense stillness, the shadows of her spars flung far to the eastward by the setting sun. At that moment I was alone on her
5 decks. There was not a sound in her—and around us nothing moved, nothing lived, not a canoe on the water, not a bird in the air, not a cloud in the sky. In this breathless pause at the threshold of a long passage we seemed to be measuring our
10 fitness for a long and arduous enterprise, the appointed task of both our existences to be carried out, far from all human eyes, with only sky and sea for spectators and for judges.

There must have been some glare in the air to
15 interfere with one's sight, because it was only just before the sun left us that my roaming eyes made out beyond the highest ridges of the principal islet of the group something that did away with the solemnity of perfect solitude. The tide of darkness
20 flowed on swiftly; and with tropical suddenness a swarm of stars came out above the shadowy earth, while I lingered yet, my hand resting lightly on my ship's rail as if on the shoulder of a trusted friend. But, with all that multitude of celestial
25 bodies staring down at one, the comfort of quiet communion with her was gone for good. And there were also disturbing sounds by this time— voices, footsteps forward; the steward flitted along the main-deck, a busily ministering spirit; a hand
30 bell tinkled urgently under the poop deck.

I found my two officers waiting for me near the supper table, in the lighted cuddy. We sat down at once, and as I helped the chief mate, I
35 said: "Are you aware that there is a ship anchored inside the islands? I saw her mastheads above the ridge as the sun went down."

He raised sharply his simple face, overcharged by a terrible growth of whisker, and
40 emitted his usual ejaculations:

"Bless my soul, sir! You don't say so!"

My second mate was a round-cheeked, silent young man, grave beyond his years, I thought; but as our eyes happened to meet I detected a
45 slight quiver on his lips. I looked down at once. It was not my part to encourage sneering on board my ship. It must be said, too, that I knew very little of my officers. In consequence of certain events of no particular significance, except to
50 myself, I had been appointed to the command only a fortnight before. Neither did I know much of the hands forward. All these people had been together for eighteen months or so, and my position was that of the only stranger on board. I
55 mention this because it has some bearing on what is to follow. But what I felt most was my being a stranger to the ship; and if all the truth must be told, I was somewhat of a stranger to myself. The youngest man on board (barring the second mate),
60 and untried as yet by a position of the fullest responsibility, I was willing to take the adequacy of the others for granted. They had simply to be equal to their tasks. But I wondered how far I should turn out faithful to that ideal conception
65 of one's own personality every man sets up for himself secretly.

Meantime the chief mate, with an almost visible effect of collaboration on the part of his round eyes and frightful whiskers, was trying
70 to evolve a theory of the anchored ship. His dominant trait was to take all things into earnest consideration. He was of a painstaking turn of mind. As he used to say, he "liked to account to himself" for practically everything that came
75 in his way, down to a miserable scorpion he had found in his cabin a week before. The why and the wherefore of that scorpion—how it got on board and came to select his room rather than the pantry (which was a dark place and more what a scorpion
80 would be partial to), and how on earth it managed to drown itself in the inkwell of his writing desk— had exercised him infinitely.

The ship within the islands was much more easily accounted for.

CONTINUE ▶

1   1

11

The tone of the first paragraph (lines 1–13) is primarily one of

A) reflective anticipation.

B) anxious dread.

C) unrestrained excitement.

D) objective analysis.

12

The reference to "some glare" (line 14) serves primarily to make the point that

A) the mastheads of another ship were not immediately visible.

B) the weather was about to change.

C) the ocean around the ship was choppy.

D) the crew was eager to get into the open sea.

13

In lines 20–24 ("The tide . . . friend") the narrator describes

A) signs of impending danger.

B) reflections of his deep inner turmoil.

C) objects of wistful contemplation.

D) the recollection of a tragic experience.

14

The captain is portrayed primarily as

A) self-conscious and diffident.

B) rugged and adventurous.

C) anxious and short-tempered.

D) scholarly yet intimidating.

15

Which choice provides the strongest evidence for the answer to the previous question?

A) Lines 4–5 ("At that moment . . . her decks")

B) Lines 24–27 ("But, with . . . for good")

C) Lines 48–51 ("In consequence . . . fortnight before")

D) Lines 63–66 ("But I . . . himself secretly")

16

In line 55, "bearing" most nearly means

A) direction.

B) demeanor.

C) relevance.

D) endurance.

17

In line 70, "evolve" most nearly means

A) change slowly.

B) ponder strenuously.

C) persuade earnestly.

D) advance randomly.

18

The "truth" to which the narrator refers in lines 57 is his

A) skepticism about his crew's ability.

B) apprehension about a dangerous voyage.

C) lack of self-confidence.

D) sense that he may be going insane.

CONTINUE

19

In line 82, "exercised" most nearly means

A) practiced.

B) strengthened.

C) utilized.

D) disquieted.

20

The "collaboration" (line 68) refers to an act of

A) selfless assistance.

B) deliberate menace.

C) contrived deceit.

D) strained contemplation.

21

The chief mate believed that, compared to the recently discovered ship, the "scorpion" (line 75) was

A) less explicable.

B) more frightening.

C) more ominous.

D) less miserable.

CONTINUE

Questions 22–32 are based on the following passages.

Passage 1 is from Lindsay Smith-Doyle, *"Thoughts on the Value of Life."* ©2015 by College Hill Coaching. Passage 2 is from C. F. Black, "Who's Afraid of Cloning?" ©2015 by College Hill Coaching. Since 1996, when scientists at the Roslin Institute in England cloned a sheep from the cells of another adult sheep, many have debated the ethics of cloning human cells. These passages are excerpts from arguments on this issue.

Passage 1

How should human life be bestowed? With human cloning looming as a real scientific
Line possibility, we must question the provenance of this ultimate gift. Our intimate participation in
5 the creation of life must never be misconstrued as control. Rather, our attitude toward the creation of life must be one of humility.

The idea of "outsourcing" the creation of human life, of relegating it to a laboratory, of
10 reducing the anticipation of childbirth to a trip to the mall or a selection from a catalog, mocks the profundity of life. The mystery is replaced by design and control. Should we turn our noses up at the most precious gift in the universe, only to
15 say: "Sorry, but I think I can do better?"

Cloning is the engineering of human life. We have for the first time the ability to determine the exact genetic makeup of a human being. Whether you believe in evolution or creationism, cloning
20 thwarts an essential step of the conception process: randomness in the case of natural selection, and guided purpose in the case of creationism. A child can be created that is no longer uniquely human but the end product of an
25 assembly line, with carefully designed and tested features. Are the astonishing processes of nature somehow deficient?

If human cloning becomes acceptable, we will have created a new society in which the value of
30 human life is marginalized. Industries will arise that turn human procreation into a profitable free-market enterprise. The executive boards of these companies will decide the course of human

evolution, with more concern for quarterly profit
35 reports than for the fate of humanity.

These are not idle concerns. Even as we ponder the ethical implications of human cloning, companies are forging ahead with procedures to clone human cells for seemingly beneficial
40 purposes, marching steadily toward a Brave New World in which humanity will be forever less human.

Passage 2

The breathless fears about human cloning should not surprise anyone who knows the
45 history of science. Every step in human progress is met with close-mindedness that often verges on paranoia. Not even medicine is spared. As doctors toil to save, prolong, and improve lives, the uninformed rage at the arrogance of science.
50 Before the merits of surgery and vaccination became commonplace and obvious, many refused to believe that cutting flesh or introducing degraded germs could do more good than harm. Perhaps we should turn from science and return to
55 superstition and magic spells?

At first glance, it might seem that cloning is a whole new ballgame. After all, cloning is "the engineering of human life," isn't it? It is the mass production of designer babies. It is the end of
60 evolution, or at least the beginning of its corporate management. It is certainly a slap in the face of God. Or is it?

Cloning foe Jeremy Rifkin is afraid of nothing so much as duplication: "It's a horrendous crime to
65 make a Xerox of someone. You're putting a human into a genetic straitjacket." The horror! I wonder how Mr. Rifkin would feel at the annual Twins Days Festival in Twinsburg, Ohio. Genetic Xeroxes everywhere!
70 Identical twins are not monsters. Rifkin's fear is vacuous. Each identical twin has his or her own unique thoughts, talents, experiences, and beliefs. Mr. Rifkin must learn that human beings are more than just their DNA; they are the
75 products of the continual and inscrutably complex interactions of environment and biology. Human clones would be no different.

"But you are playing God!" we hear. It is the cry of all whose power is threatened by the march

CONTINUE ▶

80 of human progress. It is the reasoning of the Dark
Ages, used to keep the subservient masses in their
place. Every great step humanity has ever taken
has disrupted the "natural order." Should we be
shivering in caves, eating uncooked bugs, and
85 dying of parasites, as nature intended?

But perhaps procreation is different—more
sacred. Then why have the technologies of fertility
enhancement, in vitro fertilization, embryo
transfer, and birth control become so widely
90 accepted? Each of these technologies was met at
first with legions of strident opponents. But over
time, reality and compassion overcame unreason
and paranoia. Familiarity dissipates fear.

These supposedly "moral" objections are
95 in fact impeding moral progress. With genetic
engineering, cloning, and stem cell research,
scientists finally have within their grasp
technologies that can provide ample food for
a starving world, cure devastating illnesses,
100 and replace diseased organs. Only ignorant
superstition stands in their way.

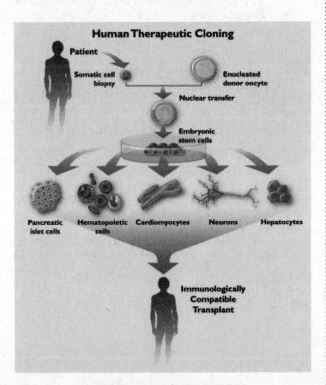

Image courtesy of NIH/NHGRI

22

In line 13, "control" refers specifically to control
over

A) the effects of cloning.

B) the development of genetic technologies.

C) the process of conception.

D) the ethical debate about cloning.

23

In Passage 1, the author's attitude toward
"outsourcing" (line 8) is one of

A) grudging approval.

B) blunt disdain.

C) firm support.

D) ironic detachment.

24

The quotations in line 15 and line 78 are similar in
that both

A) represent the opinions of cloning opponents.

B) indicate cautious advocacy for genetic
engineering.

C) are presented as being insincere.

D) contradict the viewpoints of the respective
authors.

CONTINUE

25

Jeremy Rifkin (line 63) would most likely advocate

A) the "humility" mentioned in line 7.

B) the "design and control" mentioned in line 13.

C) the "engineering" mentioned in line 16.

D) the "industries" mentioned in line 30.

26

The diagram best illustrates

A) the "guided purpose" (line 22).

B) the "assembly line" (line 25).

C) the "course of human evolution" (lines 33–34).

D) the "procedures" (line 39).

27

In line 53, "introducing" refers to an act of

A) explanation.

B) proposition.

C) announcement.

D) injection.

28

The author of Passage 1 would most likely regard the "management" (line 61) described in Passage 2 as

A) a necessary measure to avoid the abuse of procreative technologies.

B) an acceptable means by which the medical community can find alternatives to cloning.

C) a regrettable invasion of commercial interests into human reproduction.

D) a dangerous impediment to the development of effective cloning techniques.

29

Passage 2 quotes Jeremy Rifkin in lines 64–66 primarily to

A) exemplify an untenable position.

B) illustrate the potential dangers of cloning.

C) reveal the interests of the corporate community.

D) cite a corroborating opinion from an expert.

CONTINUE

1

1

30

Passage 2 refers to the Twin's Days Festival in line 68 as an example of

A) a movement that promotes beneficial cloning.

B) a seemingly harmless event that harbors hidden dangers.

C) the innocuousness of genetic duplication.

D) the logical consequences of procreative technologies.

31

The author of Passage 2 would most likely argue that the "procedures" (line 39) to which the author of Passage 1 objects are in fact

A) inconsequential aspects of the cloning debate.

B) necessary contributions to medical progress.

C) not representative of the methods used by real genetic researchers.

D) ways of manipulating public opinion.

32

Which choice provides the strongest evidence for the answer to the previous question?

A) Lines 59–61 ("It is the end . . . management")

B) Lines 71–73 ("Each identical . . . beliefs")

C) Lines 80–82 ("It is the reasoning . . . place")

D) Lines 95–100 ("With genetic . . . organs")

CONTINUE

Questions 33–42 are based on the following passage.

This passage is from Steven Pinker, *An Invitation to Cognitive Science* (Gleitman, Liberman, and Osherson, eds.) ©1995 by Bradford Book.

Language is the main vehicle by which we know about other people's thoughts, and the two
Line must be intimately related. Every time we speak we are revealing something about language, so
5 the facts of language structure are easy to come by; these data hint at a system of extraordinary complexity. Nonetheless, learning a first language is something every child does successfully, in a matter of a few years and without the need for
10 formal lessons. With language so close to the core of what it means to be human, it is not surprising that children's acquisition of language has received so much attention.

Is language simply grafted on top of cognition
15 as a way of sticking communicable labels on thoughts? Or does learning a language somehow mean learning to think in that language? A famous hypothesis, outlined by Benjamin Whorf, asserts that the categories and relations that
20 we use to understand the world come from our particular language, so that speakers of different languages conceptualize the world in different ways. Language acquisition, then, would be learning to think, not just learning to talk.

25 This is an intriguing hypothesis, but virtually all modern cognitive scientists believe it is false. Babies can think before they can talk. Cognitive psychology has shown that people think not just in words but also in images and
30 abstract logical propositions. And linguistics has shown that human languages are too ambiguous and schematic to use as a medium of internal computation: when people think about "spring," surely they are not confused as to whether they
35 are thinking about a season or something that goes "boing"—and if one word can correspond to two thoughts, thoughts can't be words.

But language acquisition has a unique contribution to make to this issue. It is virtually
40 impossible to show how children could learn a language unless you assume they have a

considerable amount of nonlinguistic cognitive machinery in place before they start.

All humans talk but no house pets do, no
45 matter how pampered, so heredity must be involved. But a child growing up in Japan speaks Japanese whereas the same child brought up in California would speak English, so environment is also crucial. Thus there is no question about
50 whether heredity or environment is involved in language, or even whether one or the other is "more important." Instead, language acquisition might be our best hope of finding out how heredity and environment interact. We know
55 that adult language is intricately complex, and we know that children become adults. Therefore something in the child's mind must be capable of attaining that complexity. Any theory that posits too little innate structure, so that its hypothetical
60 child ends up speaking something less than a real language, must be false. The same is true for any theory that posits too much innate structure, so that the hypothetical child can acquire English but not, say, Bantu or Vietnamese.

65 And not only do we know about the output of language acquisition, we know a fair amount about the input to it, namely, parents' speech to their children. So even if language acquisition, like all cognitive processes, is essentially a "black
70 box," we know enough about its input and output to be able to make precise guesses about its contents.

The study of language acquisition began around the same time as the birth of cognitive
75 science, in the late 1950s. We can see now why that is not a coincidence. The historical catalyst was Noam Chomsky's review of Skinner's *Verbal Behavior* in 1959. At that time, Anglo-American natural science, social science, and philosophy had
80 come to a virtual consensus about the answers to the questions listed above. The mind consisted of sensorimotor abilities plus a few simple laws of learning governing gradual changes in an organism's behavioral repertoire. Therefore,
85 language must be learned; it cannot be a module; and thinking must be a form of verbal behavior, since verbal behavior is the prime manifestation of "thought" that can be observed externally. Chomsky argued that language acquisition falsified

CONTINUE

1
1

90 these beliefs in a single stroke: children learn languages that are governed by highly subtle and abstract principles, and they do so without explicit instruction or any other environmental clues to the nature of such principles. Hence language
95 acquisition depends on an innate, species-specific module that is distinct from general intelligence. Much of the debate in language acquisition has attempted to test this once-revolutionary, and still
100 controversial, collection of ideas. The implications extend to the rest of human cognition.

33

This passage as a whole is primarily concerned with

A) delineating the general principles of linguistics.

B) comparing the structural qualities of various languages.

C) exploring academic questions about how we learn language.

D) examining the claims of one influential linguist.

34

The "data" mentioned in line 6 most likely include information regarding

A) the literacy levels of various countries.

B) methods for teaching infants to speak.

C) the syntax rules of different languages.

D) the structures of the human cerebral cortex.

35

In line 2, "the two" refers to

A) self and other.

B) thinking and expressing.

C) grammar and syntax.

D) learning and teaching.

36

In line 15, "sticking" most nearly means

A) applying.

B) upholding.

C) piercing.

D) maintaining.

CONTINUE ▶

37

The author's attitude toward Whorf's "hypothesis" (line 18) is best described as

A) dismissive.

B) supportive.

C) ambivalent.

D) antagonistic.

38

The statement "Babies can think before they can talk" (line 27) is intended to indicate that

A) learning to talk is much more cognitively challenging than most people believe.

B) skills associated with basic reasoning are not dependent on verbal communication.

C) both physical and cognitive skills tend to develop according to rigid timelines.

D) researchers sometimes do not take into account the particular needs of infants.

39

Which if the following best summarizes the author's view on human language acquisition?

A) Learning a language is a crucial step in learning to think, because thinking is verbal behavior.

B) The structures for learning language seem to be much simpler than what scientists previously thought.

C) Humans are born with very intricate cognitive structures for learning language.

D) Environmental input is more important than heredity in language acquisition.

40

Which choice provides the strongest evidence for the answer to the previous question?

A) Lines 1–3 ("Language is . . . intimately related")

B) Lines 23–24 ("Language acquisition . . . to talk")

C) Lines 61–64 ("The same . . . Vietnamese")

D) Lines 95–97 ("Hence language . . . general intelligence")

1   **1**

41

In line 62, "structure" refers to

A) the grammatical rules of a language.

B) the functional organization of the mind.

C) the environment in which infants learn.

D) the systems for investigating linguistic claims.

42

The subjects listed in lines 78–80 are given as examples of disciplines that, in 1959,

A) accepted the hypothesis that cognition depends on verbal skills.

B) considered the scientific method inadequate to the study of language acquisition.

C) regarded most of the processes in involved in language acquisitions to be innate.

D) questioned the conventional theories regarding how humans learn language.

CONTINUE

Questions 43–52 are based on the following passage and supplementary material.

This passage is from A. R. Kirchoff, "*The New Ecosystems of the Anthropocene*" ©2017 by College Hill Coaching.

Scavengers—animals that feed on carcasses, rotting plants, or waste—get a bad rap.
Line Yellowjackets and raccoons swarming around garbage cans can seem like annoying pests at best
5 and germ-infested monsters at worst. Indeed, scavengers have been known to spread diseases such as meningitis, leptospirosis, and bubonic plague, so it's no surprise that they are the focus of a huge extermination industry. But our habit of
10 eradicating irksome species ignores an important fact: scavenger relationships are essential to all complex life.

The selective pressures of scavenger behavior accelerate the evolution of social intelligence. For
15 thousands of generations, some scavenger species have struggled to outwit the wily hunters with whom they compete for scraps. They must predict, plan, and communicate as they approach a carcass in order to avoid becoming the next prey. At
20 the same time, hunters like *Homo sapiens* had to become more clever to protect their meat from these thieves. This social interaction has allowed at least one scavenger species to thrive in an
25 anthropocentric[1] world: *Canis lupus familiaris*—the domesticated dog. Your pet terrier would not be such a faithful companion if its ancestor, the grey wolf, had not spend so much time picking over the trash of our hunter forebears. In just 20,000
30 years, we have become symbionts,[2] turning a few lines of wolves from freeloading foragers into friendly Frisbee-fetchers.

Even less perspicacious scavengers play a vital role in complex ecosystems, often in unexpected
35 ways. As plastic waste accumulates rapidly in the ocean (and is expected to surpass the total mass of fish by 2050), and toxic chemical waste continues to be dumped into our water supplies, the role of
40 one particular class of scavenger, the *decomposers*, has become critical. These creatures break down complex molecules into simpler ones in a process called *biodegradation*. *Alcanivorax borkumensis*, a naturally occurring marine bacterium, can
45 digest petroleum and convert it into food energy. Hydrocarbons like petroleum and plastics are energy-rich organic molecules much like starches, fats, and proteins, so the idea that they can be
50 used as food by opportunistic organisms is not so biochemically far-fetched. After crude oil spills, cleanup crews encourage this biodegradation by using chemical dispersant to break the petroleum into smaller droplets, thereby creating more
55 surface area for the bacteria to attack. Another decomposer, *Aspergillus tubingensis*, is able to greatly accelerate the breakdown of polyester polyurethane, a petroleum product and one of the more durable plastics in our landfills and oceans.
60 Although environmentalists have yet to discover a practical method for harnessing *A. tubingensis* in large-scale waste mitigation systems, such biotechnological solutions may not be far off.

65 Our dependence on unicellular opportunists goes deeper still: our digestive processes, blood pressure, and immune system depend on thousands of species of scavenger bacteria that live primarily in our gut and make up our
70 *microbiome*. These organisms patrol the intricate chemical pathways of the gut and perform duties that, under normal circumstances, keep things running smoothly. The overuse of antibiotics, our favorite pharmaceutical pest-control system,
75 often compromise healthy systemic function by destroying healthful bacteria as well as harmful ones. For instance, humans with depleted levels of *Butyricicoccus pullicaecorum* in their intestines have higher rates of chronic bowel diseases like
80 ulcerative colitis and Crohn's disease. Research into how these microorganisms has exploded in recent years, particularly regarding how they interact with human chemistry to regulate our hormones, our blood sugar, and even our mood.

[1] human-centered
[2] species that live together in a mutually supportive relationship.

Plastics Generation and Recovery through Recycling in the U.S.
1960–2013

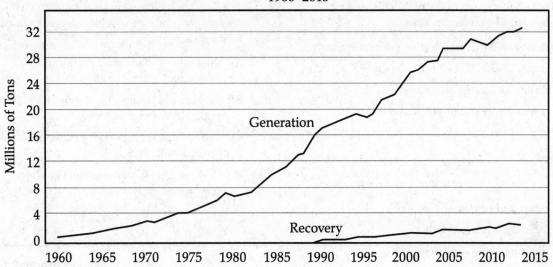

Source: U.S. Environmental Protection Acgency

43

This passage primarily serves to

A) examine several specific ecosystems that are
currently dominated by scavengers and discuss
ways of preserving those ecosystems.

B) explore various ways in which scavengers can
be beneficial to different ecosystems that are
relevant to humans.

C) explain how scavengers acquire intelligent
behavior through a long evolutionary process
involving interaction with humans.

D) discuss the ways that humans can exploit
the beneficial behaviors of scavengers while
avoiding the diseases that they spread.

44

In line 33, "perspicacious" is used to describe
scavengers that can

A) avoid predation by humans.

B) decompose complex hydrocarbons.

C) distinguish nutritious waste from toxic waste.

D) develop mutually beneficial social relationships.

45

Considering the information in the passage,
the graph would be most directly relevant to a
discussion of

A) the domestication of *Canis lupus familiaris*.

B) the proliferation of *Alcanivorax Butyricicoccus*.

C) the habitat of *Aspergillus tubingensis*.

D) the health benefits of *Butyriiccoccus
pullicaecorum*.

46

The passage indicates that the social intelligence of
scavengers enables them to

A) track increasingly elusive prey.

B) find more nutritious food sources.

C) avoid predation by clever hunters.

D) protect their food supply.

CONTINUE ▶

47

Which choice provides the best evidence for the answer to the previous question?

A) Lines 13–14 ("The selective . . . intelligence")

B) Lines 17–20 ("They must . . . prey")

C) Lines 20–22 ("At . . . thieves")

D) Lines 26–29 ("Your pet . . . forebears")

48

As used in line 41, "complex" most nearly means

A) large and intricate.

B) obscure and bewildering.

C) delicate and complicated.

D) convoluted and unfathomable.

49

As used in line 52, "encourage" most nearly means

A) inspire.

B) goad.

C) invigorate.

D) persuade.

50

The passage indicates that one hurdle to using microorganisms extensively to degrade plastic waste is that

A) they may produce toxic chemicals as a by-product.

B) they are not common to the most highly polluted ecosystems.

C) their populations are not easily controlled by environmentalists.

D) they compete with other biodegrading scavengers.

51

Which choice provides the best evidence for the answer to the previous question?

A) Lines 46–51 ("Hydrocarbons . . . far-fetched")

B) Lines 51–55 ("After . . . attack")

C) Lines 55–60 ("Another . . . oceans")

D) Lines 60–64 ("Although . . . off")

52

The last paragraph (lines 65–84) serves mainly to

A) indicate additional benefits that scavenger bacteria provide by describing how they support vital biological functions in humans.

B) provide another example of the benefits provided by microscopic scavengers by describing how bacteria enable researchers to develop better antibiotics.

C) draw a contrast to the previous discussion about the benefits of bacteria by describing some of the potential dangers of infection.

D) demonstrate how our fear of bacteria prevents us from taking full advantage of the medicinal benefits of microorganisms.

STOP

If you finish before time is called, you may check your work on this section only. Do not turn to any other section of the test.

2   2

Writing and Language Practice Test

35 MINUTES, 44 QUESTIONS

Turn to Section 2 of your answer sheet to answer the questions in this section.

2   **2**

Questions 1–11 are based on the following passage and supplementary material.

Who Really Owns American Media?

In this era of blogging, news websites, and personalized Twitter feeds, most of us believe that we have more choice than ever **1** in how we get our news. But unless you're particularly **2** apt about the world of journalism, you might be surprised to learn how few choices we really have.

Thirty years ago, 50 different corporations owned 90% of the American broadcast and news media. Today, just 6 large conglomerates **3** have the same control over that media, which is still 90%. These huge corporations have successfully lobbied the U.S. Congress to loosen or dismantle federal antitrust regulations. These regulations were designed to prevent any one corporation from driving out **4** their competition and controlling public discourse. The debate on this issue centers on the balance between liberties and governmental interference. Some argue that a corporation's freedom to acquire media and voice its opinion trumps any right the public may have to diverse points of view. **5** The other argument would be that our constitutional freedom of the press requires regulation in order to maintain a free market of ideas and an informed citizenry.

1

A) NO CHANGE
B) with getting
C) of the way we get
D) of getting

2

A) NO CHANGE
B) acute
C) savvy
D) comprehensive

3

A) NO CHANGE
B) control that same 90% of all media
C) control the same media, all 90% of it
D) are in the same 90% control of all media

4

A) NO CHANGE
B) the competition they have
C) its competition
D) it's competition

5

A) NO CHANGE
B) Others argue
C) Others would argue
D) Another being

2   2

According to data from 2007, the American media does not quite look like America. Although fully 33% of the American population was minority, **6** only 3.2% of American broadcast television outlets were controlled by minorities.

One potent antidote **7** regarding media consolidation is the Internet. **8** With some research, it reveals many resources for the curious and intelligent media consumer to hear informed voices from a wide variety of perspectives.

6

Which of the following best represents the information from Figure 1?

A) NO CHANGE

B) only 3.2% of the minority population controlled American broadcast television outlets

C) only 3.2% of the American population included minorities in control of broadcast television outlets

D) only 3.2% of American broadcast television stations were watched by minorities

7

A) NO CHANGE

B) about

C) against

D) to

8

A) NO CHANGE

B) It will reveal with some research

C) Some research will reveal

D) With some research, it will reveal

MINORITY REPRESENTATION IN BROADCAST TELEVISION

U.S. Population   U.S. Media Ownership
2007   2007

	Population	Media Ownership
African American ■	13.0%	0.6%
Hispanic American ■	15.0%	1.3%
Asian American ◻	4.5%	0.9%
Other Minority ◻	1.5%	0.4%
White Non-Minority ◻	66.0%	96.8%

Source: Freepress

CONTINUE ▶

9 Although the Web abounds with gossip, partisanship, and fear-mongering from many major outlets, and conspiracy theorists on the fringe, the careful viewer can also find thoughtful analysis and civilized debate of the issues. Sites like ProPublica, FactCheck.org, and NPR provide in-depth, nonprofit, public-supported journalism that is less influenced by any corporate or political agenda.

10 Therefore, sensationalism sells, and the media conglomerates have mastered the art. As the first great American media mogul, William Randolph Hearst, said, "If you want the public in sufficient numbers, construct a highway. Advertising is that highway." Without large advertising and lobbying budgets, these nonpartisan **11** instances of journalism will have a difficult time competing with the big boys.

9

The author wants to introduce this sentence with a representation of modern media that contrasts with the ideal of "civilized debate." Does this sentence accomplish this task?

A) Yes, because it suggests that controversial matters are ignored in modern media.

B) Yes, because it refers to relatively unsophisticated modes of conversation.

C) No, because it focuses on entertainment rather than any examination of issues.

D) No, because it refers to hypothetical situations rather than real ones.

10

A) NO CHANGE
B) Still
C) Lastly
D) In summary

11

A) NO CHANGE
B) patterns
C) receptacles
D) repositories

2   2

Questions 12–22 are based on the following passage.

The Dangers of Superstition

Have you ever knocked on wood to dodge a jinx? Do you avoid stepping on cracks in the sidewalk? Do you feel uneasy about the number 13? Most of us realize that these **12** rituals, which are based on ancient and discredited beliefs, but we can't so easily rid our minds of superstitious thinking. Every culture has its own superstitious beliefs, **13** and now anthropologists and psychologists are beginning to understand why.

Our brains constantly work to find cause-and-effect patterns in the world. When something strange happens that we can't explain, or seems to **14** collid against what we already believe, we get an uncomfortable feeling known as "cognitive dissonance." We reflexively fill this gap in knowledge with the explanations that are most easily available to us. **15** Since we are willful beings surrounded by other willful beings, and every conscious moment of our lives is filled with a sense of "agency," **16** that is: intentional action. Therefore, we imagine tiny beings living in wood, or vaporous spirits roaming the clouds that do strange or harmful things when we displease them. Willful agency is our "default" explanation.

12

A) NO CHANGE
B) rituals, that are based on
C) rituals have been based on
D) rituals are based on

13

A) NO CHANGE
B) for
C) so
D) while

14

A) NO CHANGE
B) contradict
C) disengage
D) go away from

15

A) NO CHANGE
B) Because we
C) We
D) So we

16

A) NO CHANGE
B) that is, intentional action
C) which is what intentional action is
D) which is: intentional action

CONTINUE ➡

2   **2**

[1] Our brains are creative. [2] They can design buildings, compose music, and **17** can formulate scientific theories. [3] But this creativity is sometimes hard to discipline, and so we are susceptible to strange thoughts and superstitions. [4] Many of these, like blessing people when they sneeze, are harmless if not quaint. [5] In 2014, villagers in Nigeria brought a goat into a police station, accusing it of being a witch that had attempted to steal a car and then changed into a goat. **18**

17

A) NO CHANGE
B) also can formulate
C) have formulated
D) formulate

18

The author is considering adding the following sentence to this paragraph.

> Others are sad and bizarre, such as the belief in shape-shifting.

Where should it be placed?

A) before sentence 2
B) before sentence 3
C) before sentence 4
D) before sentence 5

2

2

Although superstitious explanations relieve our cognitive dissonance, **19** it might also lead to tragedy. In 2014, people in Paraguay and Tanzania were killed because locals accused them of witchcraft. **20** Some superstitious parents have even beaten or disowned their own children because their strange behavior is attributed to demonic possession. Superstitions are also not harmless when they impede the pursuit of science, placing obstacles in the way of medical and technological breakthroughs that can improve the human condition.

Rituals intended to help your favorite football team score, like dancing or wearing your hat backward, are fun and innocuous. They **21** substitute a craving in our brains for control over situations that otherwise mystify us. **22**

19

A) NO CHANGE
B) it can
C) they can
D) they would

20

A) NO CHANGE
B) Some superstitious parents, believing that any strange behavior is a sign of demonic possession, have even beaten or disowned their own children.
C) Even beating or disowning their own children, many superstitious parents attribute their strange behavior to demonic possession.
D) Some superstitious parents, believing that their strange behavior is a sign of demonic possession, have even beaten or disowned their own children.

21

A) NO CHANGE
B) discharge
C) exempt
D) satisfy

22

Which concluding sentence is most in keeping with the content and tone of the passage as a whole?

A) However, feeling like we have control over a situation is not always the same as understanding it.
B) They represent some of humanity's greatest accomplishments, and have inspired some of our greatest works of art.
C) Centuries from now, our rituals may become so elaborate that we would scarcely recognize them as such today.
D) Without such rituals, we would not feel as connected to the people or the natural world around us.

CONTINUE

Questions 23–33 are based on the following passage.

Skepticism and the Scientific Method

Even scientists sometimes forget how essential skepticism, particularly self-skepticism, is to the scientific process. But scientific skepticism is driven by evidence, not agenda. Today, the field of climatology seems to have more than its share of skeptics, debating **23** a warming planet and the things that should be done by us about it, if anything.

24 They are coming from outside of the scientific community, many of these skeptics couch their arguments in political terms. Some claim that global warming is part of a partisan "left-wing" plot or a ploy by the scientific community to ensure funding for yet another "Chicken Little" scare. Others suggest that attempts to reduce greenhouse gas emissions by changing energy or land use policies **25** would provide a needless cost of the American taxpayer of tens to hundreds of billions of dollars annually. Some even suggest that they are really part of an international conspiracy to undermine America's competitiveness in the global marketplace.

23

A) NO CHANGE

B) what should be done about a warming planet, if we should

C) what, if anything, we should do about a warming planet

D) the things we should do about a warming planet, if we should

24

A) NO CHANGE

B) While coming

C) Their coming

D) Coming

25

A) NO CHANGE

B) would be needless in costing the American taxpayer

C) would needlessly cost the American taxpayer

D) is a needless cost to the American taxpayer of

2

2

At the same time, others who legitimately question the data or theories related to climate change are too quickly labeled right-wing "deniers," even if their concerns are not motivated by any partisan convictions.

In fact, science has, or should have, nothing to do with ideology. Rather, it **26** <u>is</u> a process of identifying significant natural phenomena, gathering evidence about those phenomena, and **27** <u>then we must find the most reliable explanation for</u> that evidence. The preponderance of the evidence suggests that the earth is getting warmer, that the effects of that warming will be problematic, that there are things we can do to prevent or at least mitigate the worst outcomes, and **28** <u>perhaps that many of these things are</u> well worth doing. There is still plenty of uncertainty about the complex systems that make up our planetary climate, but we know enough to be concerned, **29** <u>and to discuss the issue without politicizing it</u>.

26

A) NO CHANGE
B) accounts for
C) represents
D) symbolizes

27

A) NO CHANGE
B) finding the most reliable explanation for
C) then explaining in the most reliable way
D) finding the most reliable way for explaining

28

A) NO CHANGE
B) also that many of these things perhaps may be
C) many of these things perhaps may be
D) that many of these things may be

29

Which choice is most consistent with the main idea of the passage?

A) NO CHANGE
B) and to expose the agendas of those who stand in the way of saving our planet
C) but not enough to risk sacrificing our political or economic security
D) and to create a strong incentive program to transform our national energy policy

CONTINUE

The skeptics point out, rightly, that science isn't about consensus. The fact that 98% of climatologists regard something as true 30 isn't the same as it being true. After all, only centuries ago the majority of physicians worldwide believed that illnesses were caused not by germs or genetics, 31 but by demons or imbalances in "humors."

[1] Having an honest and productive conversation about global warming 32 requires an educated public. [2] When we, as public citizens, become more informed about the science of climatology, we become less susceptible to political sniping and to "consensus" as an argument. [3] Most important, perhaps, we become better able to make good decisions about the future of our nation and our planet. 33

30

A) NO CHANGE

B) won't make that true

C) would not mean it's that way

D) doesn't make it so

31

A) NO CHANGE

B) but instead from

C) but from

D) they thought it was by

32

A) NO CHANGE

B) requires the need for

C) requires our being

D) require having

33

The writer is considering adding the following sentence into this paragraph.

Furthermore, we become more adept at evaluating the facts and theories at the heart of the matter.

Where should it be placed?

A) before sentence 1

B) before sentence 2

C) before sentence 3

D) after sentence 3

2

2

Questions 34–44 are based on the following passage.

The Magic of Bohemia

Bohemia is a landlocked country in central
34 Europe, and until 1918 they were ruled from Vienna
by the Austrian Hapsburgs. Today it **35** regards a major
part of the modern Czech Republic, and its largest city,
Prague, serves as the nation's capital. Bohemia is also
another, less clearly defined country, a country of the
mind. This Bohemia in fact derives from misconceptions about the true Bohemia that go back as far as
Shakespeare, **36** designating Bohemia as the land of
gypsies and the spiritual habitation of artists.

By 1843, when Michael William Balfe's opera *The
Bohemian Girl* premiered in London, the term *Bohemian*
37 would come to mean any wandering or vagabond
soul, who need not have been associated with the arts.
The Parisian poet Henry Murger clinched the term's special association with the life of artists.

In November 1849, a dramatized version of
Murger's *Latin Quarter* tales was staged in Paris with the
title *La Vie de Bohème*. So extraordinarily successful **38**
did this prove that the stories themselves were published as *Scènes de la Vie de Bohème*. The public's appetite
was whetted and a popular cult of the gypsy-artist was
underway. Murger's volume of stories became the text-
book for the artistic life throughout the late nineteenth
and early twentieth centuries.

34

A) NO CHANGE
B) Europe, until 1918 it was ruled
C) Europe, which, until 1918, was ruled
D) Europe, having been, until 1918, ruled

35

A) NO CHANGE
B) amounts to
C) establishes
D) comprises

36

A) NO CHANGE
B) who designated Bohemia
C) he had designated Bohemia
D) being designated by him

37

A) NO CHANGE
B) had come to mean
C) came to have meant
D) had meant

38

A) NO CHANGE
B) was this proven
C) this was proved
D) this proved

CONTINUE ➡

[39] What was it that were the basic elements of this Bohemia as it evolved under Murger? To start with, Bohemia belonged to the romantic movements that preached the power of the individual imagination and came to adopt a secular religion of art. Like early Christianity, it had its true believers and its heathens. The believers in this case were the artists themselves, the elect of the spirit, touched with the divine power of imagination, while the heathen were the commercial middle classes who had [40] propagated as a result of increased commodity production in the wake of the Industrial Revolution.

[1] To the artists, these were people of no imagination who were only concerned with material things. [2] As Philistines, they seemed inhabit a different country from that of the [41] Bohemians; Murger's achievement was to define, quite persuasively, the boundaries of Bohemia in terms of a particular lifestyle. [3] In his Bohemia, the production of art was in fact less important than [42] whether one had the capacity for art. [4] Murger was also responsible for the term *Bohemian* becoming inseparably linked with the supposedly unconventional, outlandish behavior of artists, yet it is evident that he did not invent Bohemianism. [5]

39

A) NO CHANGE
B) What were they that were the basic elements
C) What basic elements were there
D) What were the basic elements

40

A) NO CHANGE
B) propitiated
C) prospered
D) preempted

41

A) NO CHANGE
B) Bohemians, Murger had the achievement of defining
C) Bohemians, but Murger's achievement was in defining
D) Bohemians; but Murger achieved defining

42

A) NO CHANGE
B) the capacity for art
C) whether one has the capacity for art
D) one's capacity of art

Most of its ingredients had existed in Paris for at least two decades before he started writing. 43

Bohemia had been a haven for the political rebel and, as the nineteenth century drew to a close, more than one French observer had seen it as the breeding-ground of cynicism, as the source of much potential danger. "It is quite clear," Jules Claretie wrote indignantly in 1888, "that every country has its Bohemians. But they do not have the influence over the rest of the nation which they do in France—thanks to that poisonous element in the French character which is known as *la blague*—or cynicism." 44

43

The writer is considering adding the following sentence to this paragraph.

> Murger can thus be described as a Bohemian of the second generation.

Where should it be placed?

A) after sentence 1

B) after sentence 2

C) after sentence 3

D) after sentence 5

44

If the author were to delete the quotation from Jules Claretie at the conclusion of this paragraph, the passage would primarily lose

A) an optimistic view of the late nineteenth-century French culture.

B) a scathing perspective on Murger's literary work.

C) a dire assessment of France's national temperament.

D) an urgent warning against a potential immigration problem.

STOP

If you finish before time is called, you may check your work on this section only.
Do not turn to any other section of the test.

5   5

Essay

50 MINUTES, 1 QUESTION

DIRECTIONS

As you read the passage below, consider how James Schlesinger uses

- evidence, such as facts or examples, to support his claims
- reasoning to develop ideas and connect claims and evidence
- stylistic or persuasive elements, such as word choice or appeals to emotion, to add power to the ideas expressed

---

Adapted from James Schlesinger, "Cold Facts on Global Warming." ©2004 by The Los Angeles Times. Originally published January 22, 2004.

1   We live in an age in which facts and logic have a hard time competing with rhetoric—especially when the rhetoric is political alarmism over global warming.

2   We continue to hear that "the science is settled" in the global warming debate, that we know enough to take significant action to counter it. Those who hold this view believe emissions of carbon dioxide are the primary cause of any change in global temperature and inevitably will lead to serious environmental harm in the decades ahead.

3   In 1997, for instance, Vice President Al Gore played a leading role in the negotiation of the Kyoto Protocol, the international agreement to deal with the fears about global warming. He was willing to embrace severe reductions in U.S. emissions, even though the Clinton administration's own Department of Energy estimated that Kyoto-like restrictions could cost $300 billion annually. Then, when it became clear that the Senate would not agree to a treaty that would harm the economy and exempt developing countries like China and India, the Clinton administration did not forward it for ratification. Since then, the treaty's flaws have become more evident, and too few countries have ratified it to allow it to "enter into force."

4   The Bush administration, as an alternative to such energy-suppressing measures, has focused on filling gaps in our state of knowledge, promoting the development of new technology, encouraging voluntary programs and working with other nations on controlling the growth of greenhouse gas emissions. Collectively, these actions involve spending more than $4 billion annually, and the U.S. is doing more than any other nation to address the climate-change issue.

5   Of these efforts, filling the gaps in our knowledge may be the most important. What we know for sure is quite limited. For example, we know that since the early 1900s, the Earth's surface temperature has risen about 1 degree Fahrenheit. We also know that carbon dioxide, a greenhouse gas, has been increasing in the atmosphere. And we know that the theory that increasing concentrations of greenhouse gases like carbon dioxide will lead to further warming is at least an oversimplification. It is inconsistent with the fact that satellite measurements over 35 years show no significant warming in the lower atmosphere, which is an essential part of the global-warming theory.

6   Much of the warming in the 20th century happened from 1900 to 1940. That warming was followed by atmospheric cooling from 1940 to around 1975. During that period, frost damaged crops in the Midwest during summer months, and glaciers in Europe advanced. This happened despite the rise in greenhouse gases. These facts, too, are not in dispute.

7   And that's just our recent past. Taking a longer view of climate history deepens our perspective. For example, during what's known as the Climatic Optimum of the early Middle Ages, the Earth's temperatures were 1 to 2 degrees warmer than they are today. That period was succeeded by the Little Ice Age, which lasted until the early 19th century. Neither of these climate periods had anything to do with man-made greenhouse gases.

8   The lessons of our recent history and of this longer history are clear: It is not possible to know now how much of the warming over the last 100 or so years was caused by human activities and how much was because of natural forces. Acknowledging that we know too little about a system as complicated as the planet's climate is not a sign of neglect by policymakers or the scientific community. Indeed, admitting that there is much we do not know is the first step to greater understanding.

9   Meanwhile, it is important that we not be unduly influenced by political rhetoric and scare tactics. Wise policy involves a continued emphasis on science, technology, engagement of the business community on voluntary programs and balancing actions with knowledge and economic priorities. As a nation, by focusing on these priorities, we show leadership and concern about the well-being of this generation and the ones to follow.

Write an essay in which you explain how James Schlesinger builds an argument to persuade his audience that the debate on global warming is unduly influenced by political alarmism. In your essay, analyze how Schlesinger uses one or more of the features listed in the box above (or features of your own choice) to strengthen the logic and persuasiveness of his argument. Be sure that your analysis focuses on the most relevant features of the passage.

Your essay should NOT explain whether you agree with Schlesinger's claims, but rather explain how Schlesinger builds an argument to persuade his audience.

CONTINUE ▶

SAT PRACTICE TEST ANSWER KEY

Section 1: Reading

1. A
2. D
3. C
4. D
5. B
6. B
7. A
8. B
9. C
10. C
11. A
12. A
13. C
14. A
15. D
16. C
17. B
18. C
19. D
20. D
21. A
22. C
23. B
24. D
25. A
26. D
27. D
28. C
29. A
30. C
31. B
32. D
33. C
34. C
35. B
36. A
37. D
38. B
39. C
40. D
41. B
42. A
43. B
44. D
45. C
46. C
47. B
48. A
49. C
50. C
51. D
52. A

Total Reading Points (Section 1)

Section 2: Writing and Language

1. A
2. C
3. B
4. C
5. B
6. A
7. D
8. C
9. B
10. B
11. D
12. D
13. A
14. B
15. C
16. B
17. D
18. D
19. C
20. B
21. D
22. A
23. C
24. D
25. C
26. A
27. B
28. D
29. A
30. D
31. A
32. A
33. C
34. C
35. D
36. B
37. B
38. A
39. D
40. C
41. A
42. B
43. D
44. C

Total Writing and Language Points (Section 2)

SAT PRACTICE TEST DETAILED ANSWER KEY

Section 1: Reading

1. **A** — Tone

In the first paragraph, the author tells us that he has little prudence and no skill in *inventing of means and methods . . . in adroit steering . . .* nor in *gentle repairing*. He also has *no skill to make money spend well*. These are *self-effacing* descriptions. They are certainly not *pontifical* (speaking as a high priest), *aspirational* (expressing high hopes and goals), or *sardonic* (grimly cynical).

2. **D** — Inference

The statement that *whoever sees my garden discovers that I must have some other garden* is the last statement in the author's list of his personal inadequacies. Therefore, this statement must be taken to be *self-effacing* as the other statements are, and specifically to mean that he lacks gardening skill.

3. **C** — Word in Context

Recall that the first paragraph begins with the question *What right have I to write on prudence . . . ?* The second provides a response to this question about his *right*: in saying *I have the same title to write on prudence as I have to write on poetry or holiness*, then, he is clearly saying that he has the *standing* or *authority* to write on prudence.

4. **D** — Inference

In following his declaration that he has the right to write on prudence (lines 13–14), Emerson states that *[w]e write from aspiration as well as from experience*. In other words, we gain the standing to write on prudence not only from expertise in prudent behavior, but also from a focused *yearning*.

5. **B** — Textual Evidence

As the explanation to the previous question indicates, the best support for this answer is in lines 13–14.

6. **B** — Specific Purpose

The sixth paragraph (lines 39–57) discusses three classes of people according to their *proficiency in knowledge of the world* (lines 39–40). The first class values *health and wealth [as] a final good* (lines 42–43). The second class values the *beauty of the symbol* (line 46–47). The third class *lives above the beauty of the symbol to the beauty of the thing signified* (lines 46–47). This last group has *spiritual perception* (line 49). Therefore, its members are superior for their ability to *discern sublime qualities*.

7. **A** — Interpretation

This phrase appears in a discussion of the individual who *traverses the whole scale* (line 50–51), that is, who has the skills of all three classes: practicality, taste, and spiritual perception. In saying that such a person *does not offer to build houses and barns* (lines 54) on the *sacred volcanic isle of nature* (lines 53–54), Emerson is saying that nature is merely a *symbol* that points to the *splendor of God* (55), and therefore not what a truly wise person chooses to fix his or her gaze upon. In other words, the building of *houses and barns* is an *unwise allegiance to worldly things*.

8. **B** — Word in Context

In saying that *the world is filled with the proverbs and acts of a base prudence* (lines 58–59), Emerson means that most of our actions and words are devoted to practical things, like the question *will it bake bread* (lines 64)? As Emerson made clear in his previous paragraph, these considerations are those of the lowest and least noble class, so theirs is an *ignoble* prudence.

9. **C** — Interpretation

As a whole, this paragraph discusses the problem that *the world is filled with the proverbs and acts of a base prudence* (lines 58–59), in other words, that our words and actions are too focused on *a devotion to matter* (lines 59–60) and its effect on our senses, *as if we possessed no other faculties than the palate, the nose, the eye and ear* (lines 60–61). Emerson describes this problem with a simile: *this is a disease like a thickening of the skin until the vital organs are destroyed* (lines 64–66). To Emerson, then, the *disease* is the problem of *sensuousness* (devotion to the senses rather than the intellect).

10. **C** — Characterization

In line 20, Emerson defines prudence as *the virtue of the senses*, but he regards the *world of the senses [as] a world of shows* (lines 22–23), that *is false when detached* (line 35) from *the thing signified* (line 47) by the natural, sensory, intellectual world, that is, from *the splendor of God* (lines 55). Furthermore, he says that prudence is *a devotion to matter, as if we possessed no other faculties than the palate, the nose, the touch, the eye and ear* (lines 59–61). Therefore, as a whole, the passage characterizes prudence as a *pursuit of practical skills and sensory experience*.

11. A — Tone

The opening paragraph describes *this breathless pause at the threshold of a long passage* (lines 8–9) in which the narrator and his crew *seemed to be measuring our fitness for a long and arduous enterprise* (lines 9–10). This describes the *reflective anticipation* of a journey. Notice that this description provides no evidence of *anxiety* or *excitement*. In fact, the scene is described in peaceful terms, with the ship *very still in an immense stillness* (line 2).

12. A — Specific Purpose

The narrator states that *some glare in the air* (lines 14–15) prevented him from seeing sooner *something that did away with the solemnity of perfect solitude* (lines 18–19). That is, he saw something that led him to believe they were not alone. In the next paragraph, this *something* is revealed to be the mastheads of *a ship anchored inside the islands* (lines 35–36).

13. C — Specific Detail

This sentence describes the scene as the narrator surveys the *tide of darkness* and *a swarm of stars* (lines 20–21) while resting his hand on the rail of the ship as if it were *the shoulder of a trusted friend* (line 24). In the next sentence, he describes this as a moment of *quiet communion* (line 26) with the ship, now interrupted by the sight of a strange ship beyond and the *disturbing sounds* (lines 27–28) being made by the crew. In other words, this sentence describes a moment of *wistful (expressing vague longing) contemplation*. Choice (A) is incorrect because, although the *disturbing sounds* and the omen of a distant ship may seem to be *signs of impending danger*, the sentence in lines 20–24 makes no mention of these things. Choice (B) is incorrect, because this moment is described as a moment of *quiet communion*, not *deep inner turmoil*. Choice (D) is incorrect, because there is no mention of any *tragic experience*.

14. A — Characterization

Since this story is being told from the perspective of the captain, we can infer his character from the nature of his narration. In the opening paragraph, the captain states that *we seemed to be measuring our fitness for a long arduous enterprise, the point of our existences to be carried out* (lines 9–12), demonstrating that he is more *reflective* than *reactive* as a leader. Much later he says, *what I felt most was my being a stranger to the ship; and if all the truth must be told, I was somewhat of a stranger to myself . . . I wondered how far I should turn out faithful to that ideal conception of one's own personality every man sets up for himself secretly* (lines 56–66). These descriptions of reflection and self-doubt reveal the captain as being *self-conscious and diffident*.

15. D — Textual Evidence

As the explanation to question 14 shows, the best evidence for this answer can be found in lines 63–65.

16. C — Word in Context

In saying *I mention this because it has some bearing on what is to follow* (lines 55–56), the narrator means that the fact that he was *the only stranger on board* (line 54) is *relevant* to what he is about to say.

17. B — Word in Context

This sentence describes how the chief mate, described as *earnest* (line 71) *and painstaking* (72), is trying strenuously to figure out why there is another ship anchored nearby. In saying that he *was trying to evolve a theory*, the narrator means he *is pondering* (thinking) *strenuously*.

18. C — Specific Detail

The *truth* that the narrator mentions in line 57 is the fact that *I am a stranger to myself*. He later goes on to explain what he means by this: *I wondered how far I should turn out faithful to that ideal conception of one's own personality every man sets up for himself secretly* (lines 63–66). In other words, this truth is the fact that he lacks *self-confidence*.

19. D — Word in Context

In saying that *the why and the wherefore of that scorpion . . . had exercised him infinitely* (lines 76–82), the narrator means that the chief mate was using his *dominant trait . . . [of] earnest consideration* (lines 71–72) to figure out how a scorpion had made its way into his cabin. That is, the questions about the scorpion had *disquieted* (unsettled) *him infinitely*.

20. D — Textual Evidence

The *collaboration on the part of [the chief mate's] round eyes and frightful whiskers* (lines 67–68) describes his facial contortions as he deliberates about the anchored ship. In other words, it is an act of *strained contemplation*.

21. A — Interpretation

In the final line, the narrator says that *the ship within the islands was much more easily accounted for*. In other words, the scorpion was *less* easily accounted for, or *less explicable*.

22. C — Inference

The second paragraph discusses the *"outsourcing" [of] the creation of human life* (lines 8–9), so the *design and control* mentioned in line 13 refer specifically to the design and control of the *process of conception*.

23. B   **Tone**

The author of Passage 1 states that the *"outsourcing" [of] the creation of human life . . . mocks the profundity of life* (lines 8–12) and he provides no indication in the passage that he otherwise approves of it. Clearly, then, he regards it with *blunt disdain*.

24. D   **Cross-Textual Analysis**

Both of these quotations represent viewpoints with which the authors of the respective passages disagree. In Passage 1, the quotation *"Sorry, but I think I can do better"* (line 15) is from those who *turn [their] noses up at the most precious gift in the universe* (lines 13–14) much to the chagrin of the author. In Passage 2, the quotation *"But you are playing God"* (line 78) is described as *the cry of all whose power is threatened by the march of human progress*, and with whom the author clearly disagrees.

25. A   **Cross-Textual Analysis**

Jeremy Rifkin is described in Passage 2 as a *cloning foe* (line 63) who is quoted as saying *"It's a horrendous crime to make a Xerox of someone. You're putting a human into a genetic straitjacket. "* Presumably, then, he would agree that *our attitude toward the creation of life must be one of humility* (lines 6–7).

26. D   **Graphical Analysis**

The illustration shows a schematic overview of some *Therapeutic Cloning Strategies* that involve removing a somatic cell from a patient and transferring its nucleus to stem cells that can then be cultured into genetically matched tissue that can then replace diseased cells and tissues in the patient. This is an example of one of the *procedures to clone human cells for seemingly beneficial purposes* (lines 39–40) described in Passage 1. Choice (A) is incorrect because the *guided purpose* refers to a principle of creationism, which is not indicated at all in the diagram. Choice (B) is incorrect because, although the process in the diagram might resemble an assembly line, it is not the *assembly line* that could be used to create a child *that is no longer uniquely human* (lines 23–24), but *with carefully designed and tested features* (lines 25–26). Choice (C) is incorrect because the diagram does not describe the *course of human evolution*, which would need to show how humans evolved from more primitive species.

27. D   **Specific Meaning**

The process *of introducing degraded germs* (line 53) describes the basic process of vaccination, which, like *cutting flesh* (line 52) (that is, surgery), must have seemed dangerous at first, but in fact can be a life-saving technology. This process is the *injection* of vaccines.

28. C   **Inference**

In this paragraph, the author of Passage 2 describes the position of cloning foes who believe that cloning *is the end of evolution, or at least the beginning of its corporate management* (lines 59–61). The author of Passage 1 is deeply concerned that *the executive boards of these [cloning] companies will decide the course of human evolution, with more concern for quarterly profit reports than for the sake of humanity* (lines 32–35). Clearly, then, the author of Passage 1 regards this management as *a regrettable invasion of commercial interests into human reproduction*.

29. A   **Specific Purpose**

Jeremy Rifkin's belief that cloning is *a horrendous crime* (line 64) directly contradicts the thesis of Passage 2, which is that cloning and similar technologies can *provide ample food for a starving world, cure devastating illnesses, and replace diseased organs* (lines 98–100). Therefore, to the author of Passage 2, Rifkin's opinion *exemplifies an untenable* (indefensible) *position*. Choice (B) may seem plausible, since Rifkin is warning of *the potential dangers of cloning*, but notice that this cannot be the reason that the author of Passage 2 quotes Rifkin, because the passage clearly disagrees with his sentiments.

30. C   **Specific Purpose**

The author of Passage 2 mentions the *Twins Days Festival* (line 68) in order to demonstrate the absurdity of Jeremy Rifkin's statement that creating a genetic *Xerox* of a person is a *horrendous crime* (line 64). To the author of Passage 2, then, the Twins Days Festival represents *the innocuousness* (harmlessness) *of genetic duplication*, since twins are genetic duplicates, and nothing to be feared.

31. B   **Cross-Textual Inference**

The author of Passage 2 does not object to the *procedures to clone human cells for seemingly beneficial purposes* (lines 39–40), and in fact believes they are *necessary contributions to medical progress* since they potentially provide technologies to *provide ample food for a starving world, cure devastating illnesses, and replace diseased organs* (lines 98–100).

32. D   **Textual Evidence**

As the explanation to question 31 indicates, the best evidence for this answer is found in lines 95–100.

33. C   **General Purpose**

The first paragraph establishes that this passage is focused on the specific processes involved in *children's acquisition of language* (lines 12–13). Therefore, the passage is primarily concerned with *exploring academic questions about how we learn language.* Choice (A) is incorrect because the passage does not begin to *delineate the general principles of linguistics*, which is a far greater subject than simply language acquisition. Choice (B) is incorrect, because although the passage does refer to children's ability to acquire diverse languages like *English . . . Bantu or Vietnamese* (lines 63–64), it does not compare their structural qualities. Choice (D) is incorrect because, although the passage does discuss the ideas of the influential linguists Benjamin Whorf (in the second paragraph) and Noam Chomsky (in the last paragraph), these references only serve the larger purpose of exploring the questions of language acquisition, and do not serve as the overall focus of the passage.

---

34. C   Inference

In the first paragraph, the author indicates that *[e]very time we speak we are revealing something about language, so the facts of language structure are easy to come by* (lines 3–6). Therefore, the *data* mentioned in line 6 are *the facts of language structure*, which would likely include *the syntax (rules governing word order) of different languages.* Choice (A) is incorrect because information about *literacy levels* is not information about *language structure.* Choice (B) is incorrect because methods of teaching are not *facts of language structure.* Choice (D) is incorrect because, although the passage does mention the innate *structure* (line 59) of the brain a few paragraphs later, this is clearly not what line 6 is referring to.

---

35. B   Inference

The phrase *the two* (line 2) refers to two nouns in the previous clause: *language* and *thoughts*, in other words, *thinking and expressing.*

---

36. A   Word in Context

The author uses the phrase *sticking communicable labels on thoughts* (lines 15–16) to describe one particularly simplistic theory about the language acquisition. The author is using the metaphor of *applying* name tags or labels to describe one way of describing how words are used. Choice (B) is incorrect because *upholding* refers to a process of confirming an official claim or pronouncement. Choice (C) is incorrect because, although *sticking* (as with a needle) can mean *piercing*, this reference clearly does not imply any act of puncturing. Choice (D) is incorrect because this phrase describes an act of *acquisition*, that is, learning something new, rather than *maintaining* something old.

---

37. D   Tone/Attitude

After describing Benjamin Whorf's theory, the author then states that *virtually all modern cognitive scientists believe it is false* (lines 25–27). The author's ensuing discussion makes it clear that he agrees with these

cognitive scientists. That is, he is *antagonistic* toward Whorf's hypothesis. Choice (A) is wrong because the author does not *dismiss* Whorf's hypothesis, but rather regards it as *an intriguing hypothesis* which just happens to be incorrect. (To *dismiss* an idea is to believe it is not even worthy of consideration, not merely to reject it after consideration.) Choice (B) is clearly wrong because the author does not *support* Whorf's hypothesis. Choice (C) is wrong because the author does not have any conflicting feelings about the hypothesis.

---

38. B   Interpretation

The author states that *babies can think before they can talk* (line 27) in order to refute Whorf's hypothesis that we can't think in terms of *categories and relations* (line 19) until our language gives us the words to do so. Whorf believes that language precedes thought. The author of this passage is saying the opposite: that *skills associated with basic reasoning are not dependent on verbal communication.*

---

39. C   Thesis

The author's view on human language acquisition can be found in lines 95–97: *language acquisition depends on an innate, species-specific module that is distinct from general intelligence.* This module must have an intricate *innate structure* (line 59) in order to acquire a language that is itself *intricately complex* (line 55). Choice (A) is incorrect because it represents the Whorf hypothesis, which the author explicitly rejects. Choice (B) is incorrect because the author does not state that the structures for learning language are simple. Choice (D) is incorrect because the author places more emphasis on the innate structure in the brain that enables language acquisition than he does on environmental input.

---

40. D   Textual Evidence

As the explanation to question 39 indicates, the best evidence for this answer is found in lines 95–97.

---

41. B   Interpretation

Lines 58–64 discuss the author's belief that the *innate structure* in the brain dedicated to language acquisition cannot be either too simple or too complex. This kind of *structure* refers to the *functional organization of the mind.* Notice that the *structure* being discussed here is not the same as the *structure* mentioned in line 5, which refers to the structure of language itself.

---

42. A   Inference

The author states that, in 1959, *Anglo-American natural science, social science, and philosophy had come to a virtual consensus about the answers to the questions listed above* (lines 78–81), that is, the questions listed in lines 14–17: *Is language simply grafted on top of cognition as a way of sticking communicable labels on thoughts? Or does learning a language somehow mean learning to think in that language? The* consensus *on these topics was that* language must be learned; it cannot be a module; and thinking must be a form of verbal behavior *(lines 85–87) Therefore, the disciplines* accepted the hypothesis that cognition depends on verbal skills.

---

43. B General Purpose

The passage begins by saying our negative view of scavengers *ignores an important fact: scavenger relationships are essential to all complex life* (lines 10–12). The second paragraph describes how scavenger behavior drives social intelligence, as with dogs. The third describes how decomposers break down petroleum and plastics in the environment. The fourth discusses how scavenger bacteria in the human gut help to regulate our bodily systems. As a whole, then, the passage serves to *explore various ways in which scavengers can be beneficial to different ecosystems that are relevant to humans.* Choice A is wrong because the passage does not discuss *ways of preserving ecosystems.* Choice C is wrong because social intelligence is only discussed in the second paragraph. Choice D is wrong because the passage does not discuss ways of *avoiding the diseases that [scavengers] spread.*

---

44. D Word in Context

Since the previous paragraph discussed the *evolution of social intelligence* (line 14) among scavengers like the grey wolf, and their evolution into *friendly Frisbee-fetchers* (lines 31–32), the phrase perspicacious scavengers is referring to those scavengers that can *develop mutually beneficial social relationships.*

---

45. C Graphical Inference

The graph shows how much U.S. plastic is going into the environment, such as oceans and landfills, rather than being recycled. In lines 55–64, the passage discusses the ability of *Aspergillus tubingensis* to break down *polyester polyurethane, a petroleum product and one of the more durable plastics in our landfills and ocean.* Since plastics are a food source for *A. tubingensis*, the graph is appropriate to a discussion of *the habitat of Aspergillus tubingensis.*

---

46. C Inference

In lines 15–20, the passage says that *some scavenger species have struggled to outwit the wily hunters with whom they compete for scraps . . . in order to avoid becoming the next prey.* Choice A is wrong because tracking prey is a hunter behavior, not a scavenger behavior. Choice B is

wrong because the passage does not discuss how scavengers might find more nutritious food sources. Choice D is wrong because, although the passage does state that *hunters like* Homo sapiens *had to become more clever to protect their meat from these thieves* (lines 20–22), this is an intelligent behavior of hunters, not scavengers.

---

47. B Textual Evidence

As the explanation to question 46 indicates, the best evidence for this answer can be found in lines 17–20.

---

48. A Word in Context

A process of *break[ing] down complex molecules into simpler ones* (lines 41–42) implies that the original molecules are *larger and more intricate* than they will become. Choice B is wrong because *obscure and bewildering* do not describe physical properties. Choice C is wrong because the passage does not imply that these molecules are *delicate;* they just need a special process to break them down. Choice D is wrong because *unfathomable* does not describe a physical property.

---

49. C Word in Context

The phrase *encourage this biodegradation* (line 52) means *do something to invigorate the process.* Choices A, B, and D are all incorrect because *inspire, goad,* and *persuade* are verbs that can only be applied to people, not chemical processes.

---

50. C Detail

In lines 60–63, the passage indicates that *environmentalists have yet to discover a practical method for harnessing* A. tubingensis *in large-scale waste mitigation systems,* which means that these microorganisms are not easily controlled.

---

51. D Textual Evidence

As the explanation to question 50 indicates, the best evidence for this answer is found in lines 60–64.

---

52. A Purpose

The final paragraph discusses how scavenger bacteria in the human gut help to keep *things running smoothly* (lines 72–73), specifically by maintaining our *digestive processes, blood pressure, and immune system* (lines 66–67). Choice B is wrong because the paragraph cautions against the overuse of antibiotics, but does not discuss how to develop them. Choice C is wrong because the paragraph discusses benefits of bacteria, not dangers. Choice D is wrong because although this paragraph cautions against overusing antibiotics, it does not say that it is due to any *fear of bacteria.*

Section 2: Writing and Language

1. A   Idiom

The original phrasing is best. Choice (B) is incorrect because *choice with getting* is not idiomatic. Choice (C) is incorrect because *choice of the way* is not idiomatic. Choice (D) is incorrect *choice of getting*, although idiomatic conveys an illogical idea in this context.

2. C   Diction

Here we are asked to choose the best word to convey the appropriate idea in this sentence. The sentence indicates that we *might be surprised to learn* something about the world of journalism, and hence that most of us are not as informed about the world of journalism as we could be. In other words, we are not particularly *savvy* (knowledgeable) about the world of journalism. *Apt* = suitable to the circumstances; *acute* = sharp; *comprehensive* = complete.

3. B   Diction/Logic

In the original phrasing, the pronoun *which* is illogical, since it refers to *the media*: that is, saying *the media is 90%* does not make sense. Choice (C) is incorrect because the phrase *all 90% of it* is illogical: *all of it* means 100% of it. Choice (D) is incorrect because it is both unidiomatic and illogical.

4. C   Possessive Form/Pronoun Agreement

In the original phrasing, the pronoun *their* disagrees with its antecedent *corporation*, which is singular. Recall that the possessive form of the pronoun *it is its (it's = it is)*. The only choice that avoids both the agreement error and the diction error is (C).

5. B   Parallelism

This phrase should be parallel to the subject-verb pair in the previous sentence, *Some argue*. The only choice with a parallel verb form is (B).

6. A   Data Analysis

The original phrasing is the only option that represents the data in Figure 1 accurately. Since the second circle graph represents all broadcast television media and its ownership, it indicates that 3.2% (0.6% + 1.3% + 0.9% + 0.4%) of American broadcast television outlets were controlled by minorities.

7. D   Idiom

The idiomatic form of this phrase is *antidote to*.

8. C   Clear Expression/Pronoun Antecedents

In choices (A), (B), and (D), the pronoun *it* lacks any clear referent. The only choice that avoids this problem is (C).

9. B   Cohesiveness/Purpose

Examples that contrast *civilized debate* would have to be examples of *uncivilized* debate. *Gossip* and *fear-mongering* certainly qualify as relatively *uncivilized* and *unsophisticated* forms of discourse.

10. B   Idiom, Pronoun-Antecedent Agreement

Here, we are looking for the most appropriate logical transition from the previous paragraph to the new one. The last sentence of the previous paragraph gave examples of *in-depth, nonprofit, public-supported journalism that is less influenced by any corporate or political agenda*. The new paragraph, however, begins with a discussion of *sensationalism* and how it *sells*, which provides a stark contrast to the previous paragraph. This requires a contrasting coordinator, such as *nevertheless* or *still*.

11. D   Diction/Clear Expression of Ideas

We want a word to represent the websites like ProPublica and NPR, as mentioned in the previous paragraph, that engage in relatively noncorporate and apolitical journalism. The phrase *instances of journalism* indicates specific articles or broadcasts, rather than the organizations themselves. The phrase *patterns of journalism* indicates trends in those articles or broadcasts, rather than the organizations themselves. The phrase *receptacles of journalism* indicates containers that receive journalism rather than organizations that produce it. Only (D) *repositories of journalism* provides a phrase that refers to the organizations themselves.

12. D   Coordination/Verb Tense

The original phrasing creates a sentence fragment rather than an independent clause. Choice (B) is incorrect because it commits the same error. Choices (C) and (D) both form independent and idiomatic clauses, but choice (C) is incorrect because the sentence is clearly making a claim about the *current state of being* of these rituals, rather than the *current status-as-consequence* of these rituals, so the present perfect (or "present consequential") form is not appropriate. (For more on using the "perfect" or "consequential" aspect, see Chapter 4, Lesson 23.)

13. A   Coordination/Conjunctions

The original phrasing is best. Choice (B) is incorrect because the second clause does not explain the first. Choice (C) is incorrect because the second clause does not follow as a consequence of the first. Choice (D) is incorrect because there is no tonal or semantic contrast between the clauses.

14. B   Diction/Clear Expression of Ideas

The phrase *collide against* is not idiomatic: *collide with* is the correct idiom, although this phrase would imply more of a physical relationship than the sentence intends. Since the sentence indicates a conflict between an *event* and a *belief* so the verb should express a relationship between *ideas*, rather than *objects*. Of the choices, only (B) *contradict* serves this purpose effectively.

15. C   Coordination

In this sentence, the conjunction *and* establishes the relationship between the coordinate independent clauses, so any subordinating conjunction like *since, so,* or *because* is inappropriate.

16. B   Diction, Agreement

Colons must always follow independent clauses, so choices (A) and (D) are incorrect. This phrase must provide a definition of the term "agency," which is precisely what choice (B) *that is, intentional action* does. Choice (C) is incorrect because it categorizes rather than defines.

17. D   Parallelism

This sentence presents a list of present tense verbs: *design . . . compose . . . and formulate.* The original phrasing is incorrect because it reinserts the auxiliary *can*, which breaks the parallel structure of the list. Only choice (D) maintains this parallel form.

18. D   Cohesiveness

This sentence belongs before sentence 5, because it provides a parallel idea to the one presented in sentence 4. Sentence 4 states that *Many of these [superstitions] are harmless if not quaint,* so the next sentence should provide a transition to some of the less pleasant aspects of superstitious thinking.

19. C   Pronoun-Antecedent Agreement/Verb Mood

In the original phrasing, the pronoun *it* does not agree with its plural antecedent *explanations*; therefore, choices (A) and (B) are incorrect. Choice (D) is incorrect because the auxiliary *would* implies necessity, rather than ability, which is illogical in this context.

20. B   Clear Expression/Pronoun Antecedents

The original phrasing is incorrect because the two instances of the pronoun *their* have conflicting antecedents, and the second clause is needlessly in the passive voice. Choices (C) and (D) have similar pronoun referent problems. Only choice (B) is phrased without ambiguous pronouns.

21. D   Diction

The previous sentence, as well as the passage as a whole, indicates that superstitious rituals are used to *satisfy a craving in our brains for control.*

22. A   Cohesiveness

Only choice (A) maintains the skeptical and analytical tone toward superstitious rituals that is established in the rest of the passage.

23. C   Clear Expression

The original phrasing is incorrect because the phrase *debating a warming planet* is illogical: only *theories, claims,* or *ideas* can be topics of debate. Choices (B) and (D) are incorrect because the clause *if we should* lacks a logical object.

24. D   Comma Splices/Coordination

The original phrasing is incorrect because it creates a comma splice. Two independent clauses may not be joined by only a comma. Choice (B) is incorrect because the conjunction *while* is illogical. Choice (C) is incorrect because it forms a noun phrase, which does not coordinate with any part of the main clause. Choice (D) creates a participial phrase that appropriately modifies the subject of the main clause.

25. C   Clear Expression/Idiom

In the original phrasing, the verb *provide* is used illogically and the phrase *cost of the American taxpayer* is unidiomatic. Choice (B) is incorrect because *needless in costing* is unidiomatic. Choice (D) is incorrect because the verb *is* disagrees in number with its subject *attempts.*

26. A   Diction

The original phrasing is best. The verb *is* serves most effectively in the role of defining *science.*

27. B   Parallelism

The underlined phrase is the third item in a parallel list: *identifying . . . gathering . . . and finding.* Choice (B) best maintains this parallel structure without introducing any other error. Choice (D) provides a parallel form, but the phrase *way for explaining* is unidiomatic.

28. D   Parallelism

The underlined phrase is part of a parallel list: *that the earth . . . that the effects . . . that there are things . . . and that many of these things . . .* Only choice (D) maintains this parallel structure.

29. A   Logical Cohesiveness

The original phrasing best, since the passage is about eliminating politics and ideology from discussions about climate change. The other choices insert points of advocacy that conflict with the tone and purpose of the passage as a whole.

---

30. D — Clear Expression of Ideas/Verb Mood/Verb Tense

The original phrasing includes an illogical core: *the fact . . . isn't the same as it being true.* Choice (B) is incorrect because a statement of general fact should not be in the future tense. Choice (C) is incorrect because a statement of general fact should not be in the subjunctive mood. Choice (D) uses the idiom *make it so* logically and grammatically.

---

31. A — Parallelism

The original phrasing is the only option that completes the parallel construction *caused not by germs . . . but by demons.*

---

32. A — Verb Form/Clear Expression

The original phrasing is the most logical and concise.

---

33. C — Logical Coherence

The adverb *furthermore* indicates that this sentence is extending a line of reasoning. Since it clearly follows the parallel clauses of sentence 2, *When we . . . become . . . we become . . .* and therefore it most logically follows sentence 2 but precedes sentence 3.

---

34. C — Pronoun Agreement/Verb Aspect

The original phrasing is incorrect because the pronoun *they* disagrees in number with the antecedent *Bohemia.* Choice (B) is incorrect because it produces a comma splice. Choice (D) is illogical because the use of the present perfect participle *having been* improperly implies a consequence.

---

35. D — Diction

The original phrasing is illogical because a country cannot *regard* (consider in a particular way; concern) anything. This verb must show a relationship between a particular country and a particular geographical region. Only choice (D) *comprises* (makes up) expresses this relationship in a logical way.

---

36. B — Coordination

The original phrasing is incorrect because it creates a dangling participle: the participle *designating* does not share its subject with the main clause. Choice (C) is incorrect because it creates a comma splice. Choice (D) is incorrect because it also creates a dangling participle. Choice (B) is best because it avoids both the comma splice and dangling participle.

---

37. B — Verb Tense/Verb Aspect

The phrase *by 1843* indicates that the status of the term *Bohemian* had become established prior to that point in time. Therefore, the verb requires the *past perfect* or *past consequential* form: *had come to mean.* Although choice (D) is a verb in the past consequential form, it incorrectly implies that the term no longer had that particular meaning in 1843.

---

38. A — Coordinating Modifiers

This sentence is trying to convey the fact that *[La Vie de Bohème]* proved *[to be so]* extraordinarily successful that the stories themselves were published. This requires the active voice, so choices (B) and (C) are incorrect. Choice (D) is incorrect because it is unidiomatic.

---

39. D — Number Shift

The original phrasing is incorrect because of the number shift between *it* and *elements.* Choices (B) and (C) are needlessly wordy. Choice (D) is clear and concise.

---

40. C — Diction/Logical Coherence

This sentence indicates the effect that *increased commodity production* had on the *commercial middle class.* It is illogical to say that the middle class *propagated* (was transmitted), *propitiated* (won the favor of someone), or *preempted* (took action to prevent something) as a result of this increased production. It is, however, logical to say that the middle class *prospered* (flourished) as a result of it.

---

41. A — Coordination of Clauses

The original phrasing best coordinates the two related, but independent, clauses. Choice (B) produces a run-on sentence with a comma splice. Choice (C) is illogical and unidiomatic. Choice (D) is illogical and misuses the semicolon.

---

42. B — Clarity of Expression/Parallelism

Choice (B) provides the most parallel comparison: *the production of art was in fact less important than the capacity for art.*

---

43. D — Coordination of Ideas

The use of the adverb *thus* indicates that this sentence represents a logical consequence of some particular state of affairs. That state of affairs is best indicated by sentence 5: *Most of its ingredients had existed in Paris for at least two decades before he started writing.* This explains why Murger can be described as a *Bohemian of the second generation.*

---

44. C — Coherence/Meaning

This question is essentially asking us to describe the function of Claretie's quotation. Since it refers to a *poisonous element in the French character,* it is clearly indicating a *dire assessment of France's national temperament.*

Section 3: Essay

Sample Response

James Schlesinger's essay, "Cold Facts on Global Warming," is a counterargument to the "political alarmism" (to use Schlesinger's words) over global warming. His tone is critical but sober, and he makes frequent use of carefully selected scientific and historical data, juxtaposed with hints at the dangers of political posturing, to make the case for caution in addressing the issue of climate change. He appeals frequently to the ethics of economic prudence and global stewardship, as well as the value of scientific judiciousness. Unfortunately, because Schlesinger's essay was written over a decade ago, it lacks the evidence from the current golden age of climate science. More substantially, however, Schlesinger undermines his own purpose by making political criticisms while calling for nonpartisan objectivity, by mongering fearsome scenarios while arguing against "scare tactics," and by ignoring the scientific evidence against his claims while advocating an "emphasis on science."

Schlesinger begins his discussion with a call for "facts and logic" over "rhetoric." This is classic polemical posturing: we all believe that our positions are "factual and logical" and that our opponents' are merely "rhetoric." In Schlesinger's view, the "rhetoric" includes the claims that "emissions of carbon dioxide are the primary cause of any change in global temperature and inevitably will lead to serious environmental harm in the decades ahead." By inserting the modifiers "any" and "inevitably," he creates a straw man. Most who argue about the seriousness of climate change generally avoid such absolute assertions and instead present evidence from satellites, ice cores, atmospheric analysis, and comprehensive long-term climatic studies to build a case for action. Schlesinger does not address this evidence.

In his argument, Schlesinger appears to value small government and the protection of American industry over the stewardship of the planet. His concern about the Kyoto Protocol of 1997 is not that it eschews the "facts and logic" of climate science, but rather that it "could cost $300 billion annually." He presents no scientific critique of the Kyoto Protocol of 1997 beyond the assertion that Democrat Al Gore was "willing to embrace" a "treaty that would harm the economy," and the vague claim that "the treaty's flaws have become more evident." His method of argumentation here appears to contradict his call for "facts and logic" over "rhetoric."

In contrast to the irresponsibility of Al Gore and the Clinton administration, Schlesinger offers the soberly scientific Bush administration, which "focused on filling in gaps in our state of knowledge, promoting the development of new technology, encouraging volunteer programs, and working with other nations on controlling the growth of greenhouse gas emissions." Schlesinger does not offer a specific benefit our planet has gained from these efforts, which even Schlesinger himself admits involved "spending more than $4 billion annually." Someone pleading for fiscal responsibility might try to account for such a huge expenditure.

Schlesinger believes that our inaction on climate change is a virtue: that scientific prudence requires "filling the gaps in our state of knowledge" above everything else, including industrial restraint. He states that "what we know for sure is quite limited," yet is confident enough in his limited knowledge to assert that "the theory that increasing concentrations of greenhouse gases like carbon dioxide will lead to further warming is at least an oversimplification," directly contradicting the simple middle school experiment showing that a soda bottle filled with carbon dioxide warms far more quickly than one filled only with air.

Schlesinger then selects data trends that seem to support his call for caution, rather than action: he asserts that "satellite measurements over 35 years show no significant warming in the lower atmosphere" and that there was "atmospheric cooling from 1940 to around 1975." Schlesinger does not explain why climate scientists, who are certainly aware of these data, nevertheless believe in anthropogenic global warming.

Not to be accused of cherry-picking data, Schlesinger next offers "a longer view of climate history." He asserts that temperatures "were 1 to 2 degrees warmer than they are today" during the Climatic Optimum of the early Middle Ages, and this warming did not have "anything to do with man-made greenhouse gases." Evidently, we should think that because it was warmer a very long time ago, burning coal today must not be changing the climate.

In the last two paragraphs, Schlesinger essentially retracts his concern about "filling the gaps in our state of knowledge" after all, because he believes it is impossible to fill the most important gaps: "It is not possible to know now how much of the warming over the last 100 years or so was caused by human activities and how much was because of natural forces." So if it is impossible to know, we might ask, why should we expend "more than $4 billion annually" to study it? He does not say. We get Schlesinger's most sonorous call to action in the last paragraph, where he suggests "engagement of the business community on voluntary programs." That is, get big government off the backs of corporations and let them do as they please.

Scoring

Reading—4 out of 4

This response demonstrates a very strong and thorough comprehension of Schlesinger's essay through skillful use of summary, paraphrase, and direct quotations. The author summarizes Schlesinger's central tone, thesis, and modes of persuasion (*His tone is critical but sober, and he makes frequent use of carefully selected scientific and historical data, juxtaposed with hints at the dangers of political posturing, to make the case for caution in addressing the issue of climate change.*) and shows a clear understanding of how Schlesinger's supporting ideas string together and serve his overall thesis (*Schlesinger begins his discussion with a call . . . He appears to value small government . . . Schlesinger offers the soberly scientific Bush administration . . . Schlesinger believes that our inaction on global warming is a virtue . . . Schlesinger next offers . . . In the last two paragraph, Schlesinger essentially retracts his concern*). Importantly, this response also offers abundant supporting quotations to illustrate each paraphrase. Taken together, these elements demonstrate outstanding comprehension of Schlesinger's essay.

Analysis—4 out of 4

Although this response occasionally veers toward advocacy, it never turns away from careful analysis. Indeed, its thoughtful and thorough critique of Schlesinger's essay demonstrates a sophisticated understanding of the analytical task. The author has identified Schlesinger's primary modes of argument (*He appeals frequently to the ethics of economic prudence and global stewardship, as well as the value of scientific judiciousness*) and even uses those standards to analyze Schlesinger's essay itself, and indicates points at which Schlesinger's argument seems self-defeating (*Schlesinger undermines his own purpose by making political criticisms while calling for nonpartisan objectivity, by mongering fearsome scenarios while arguing against "scare tactics," and by ignoring the scientific evidence against his claims while advocating an "emphasis on science"*). Overall, this analysis of Schlesinger's essays demonstrates a thorough understanding not only of the rhetorical task that Schlesinger has set for himself, but also of the degree to which it upholds its own standards.

Writing—4 out of 4

This response demonstrates an articulate and effective use of language and sentence structure to establish and develop a clear and insightful central claim that *Schlesinger's essay is a counterargument to the "political alarmism" . . . over global warming . . .* but that *it undermines [its] own purpose.* The response maintains a consistent focus on this central claim, and supports it with a well-developed and cohesive analysis of Schlesinger's essay. The author demonstrates effective choice of words and phrasing (*undermines his own purpose . . . mongering fearsome scenarios . . . Schlesinger believes that our inaction on climate change is a virtue*), strong grasp of relevant analytical and rhetorical terms, like *economic prudence, nonpartisan objectivity,* and *polemical posturing.* The response is well-developed, progressing from general claim to specific analysis to considered evaluation. Largely free from grammatical error, this response demonstrates strong command of language and proficiency in writing.